ATLAS OF SOUTH CAROLINA

THIRD EDITION

Edited by Austin Crane, Michael Mewborne, and Jory Fleming

Maps by Elbie Bentley

Published in cooperation with the South Carolina Geographic Alliance

THE UNIVERSITY OF
SOUTH CAROLINA PRESS

CONTENTS

1 LOCATION

South Carolina is a small state, ranking fortieth among the fifty states in total area. It is situated in the southeastern United States and covers about 32,000 square miles. Today, travelers can cross the state in a few hours' time. Its north–south distance is about 225 miles and its east-west distance is about 285 miles. The state lies between 35°15′ and 32°00′ north latitude and 78°30′ and 83°30′ west longitude.

The state is often divided into three general regions: the Upstate, the Midlands, and the Lowcountry. The Upstate was called the Back Country during the Colonial period and now consists of the Blue Ridge and Piedmont landform regions. The Midlands is a newer term, used since the 1950s, that encompasses the area surrounding Columbia in central South Carolina. The Lowcountry refers to the Coastal Plain. There is no specific or generally agreed upon boundary that separates the regions.

South Carolina's size has been reduced over time since its original English charters. Eight Lords Proprietors received a grant in 1665 to the land between 29°00′ and 36°30′ north latitude that was situated between the Atlantic and Pacific Oceans. The size of the colony was reduced when it was divided into northern and southern provinces in 1729 and the colony of Georgia was created in 1732.

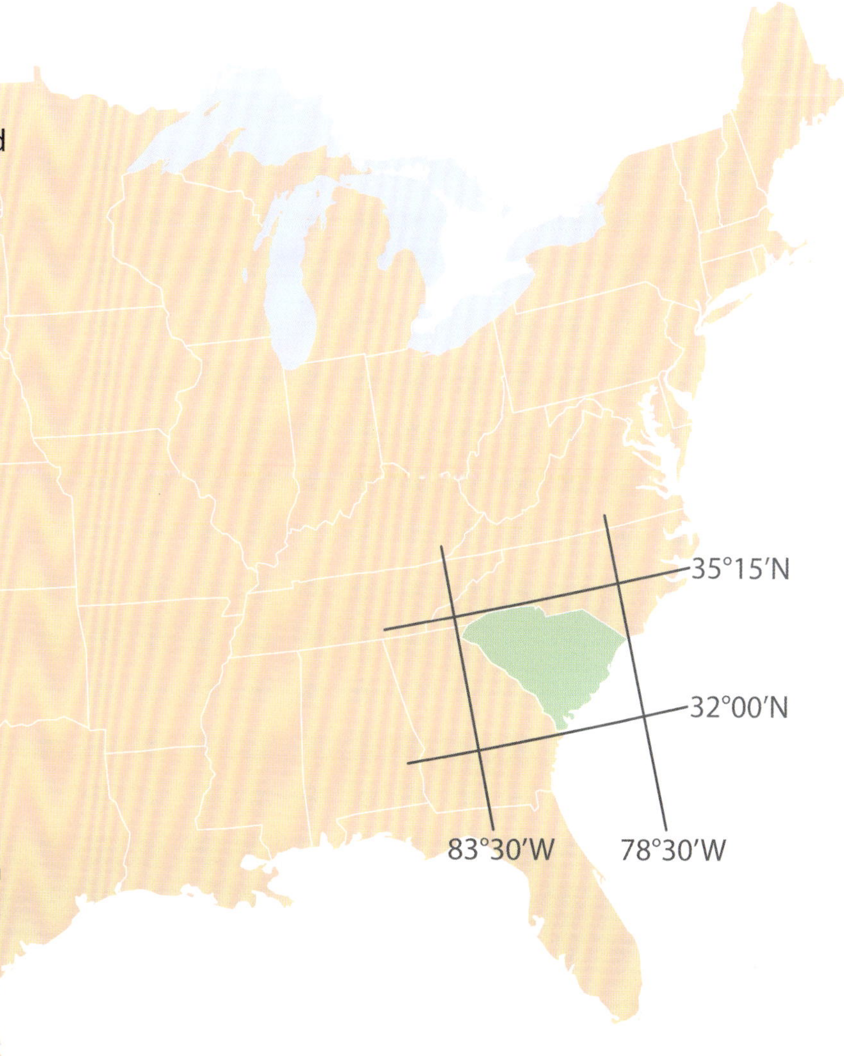

COUNTIES AND COUNTY SEATS

Politically, the state is subdivided into forty-six counties. Other political divisions have been used over the state's history. These included parishes and districts. The present county structure has existed since 1919, the last year a new county—Allendale—was created. When county boundaries are disputed, occasionally minor changes are made, like between Berkeley and Dorchester counties in 2018. The center of government for each county is called the county seat. The county seat is often the largest city or town and is typically located near the middle of the county, but not all counties follow these rules. Columbia is the county seat of Richland County and has been the state's capital city since 1786.

Robert Mills, one of the nation's early architects, designed at least eighteen county courthouses in South Carolina. His architectural style created a familiar look among many county seats. His county courthouse in Winnsboro is shown here. Mills is best known for designing the Washington Monument in Washington, DC.

2 NATURAL LANDSCAPE

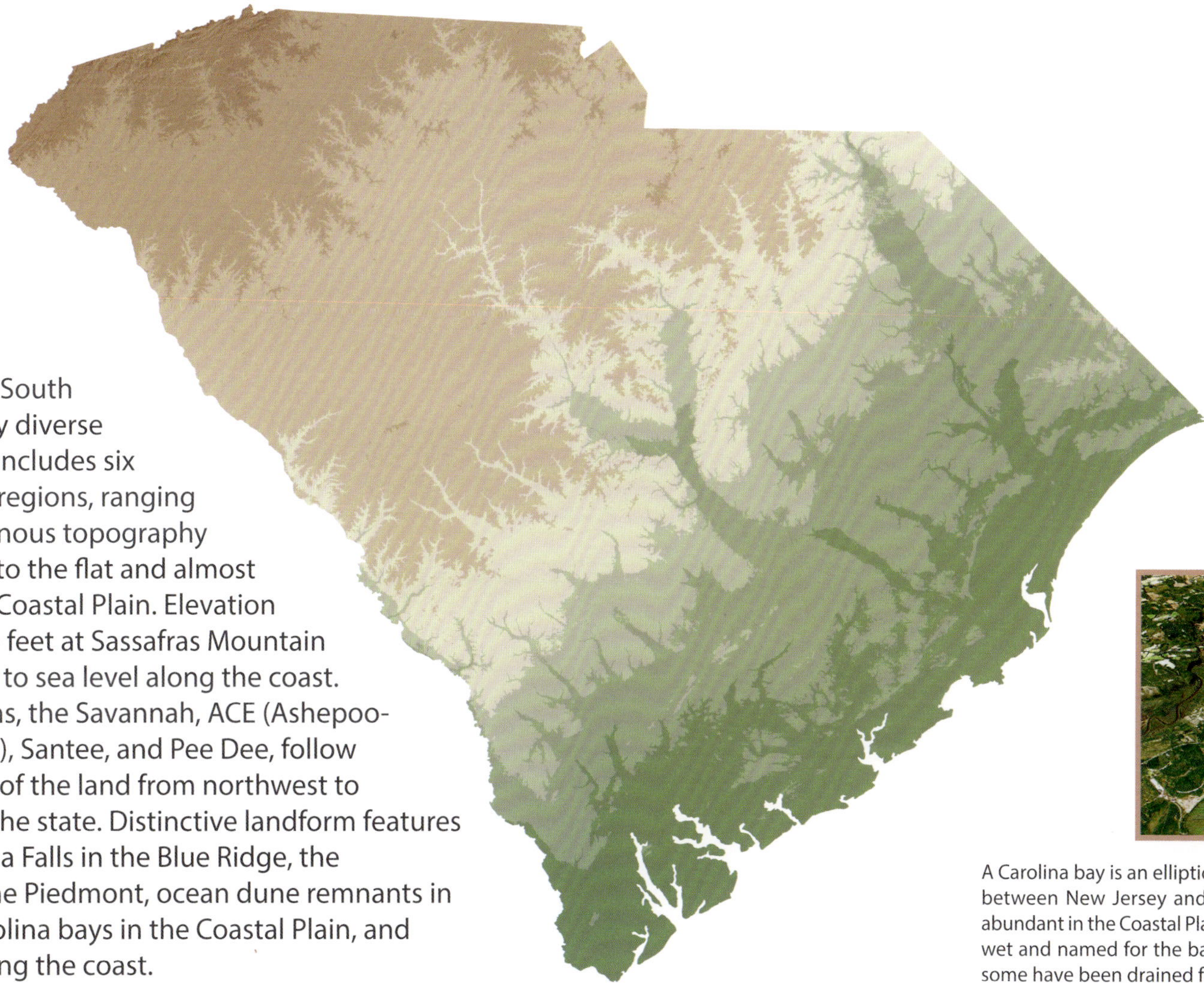

For a small state, South Carolina has a very diverse natural setting. It includes six distinct landform regions, ranging from the mountainous topography of the Blue Ridge to the flat and almost featureless Outer Coastal Plain. Elevation ranges from 3,560 feet at Sassafras Mountain in Pickens County to sea level along the coast. Major river systems, the Savannah, ACE (Ashepoo-Combahee-Edisto), Santee, and Pee Dee, follow the general slope of the land from northwest to southeast across the state. Distinctive landform features include Issaqueena Falls in the Blue Ridge, the monadnocks of the Piedmont, ocean dune remnants in the Sandhills, Carolina bays in the Coastal Plain, and barrier islands along the coast.

A Carolina bay is an elliptically shaped landform found between New Jersey and Florida, but they are most abundant in the Coastal Plain of the Carolinas. Generally wet and named for the bay trees that surround them, some have been drained for agricultural use.

LANDFORM REGIONS

Landforms are often described by their relief, or differences in elevation, across space. Taken together, individual landform features such as mountains can be grouped into landform regions. Broad landform regions in the United States separate mountains from plateaus and highlands from plains. South Carolina consists of land within both the Appalachian Highlands and the Atlantic Plain.

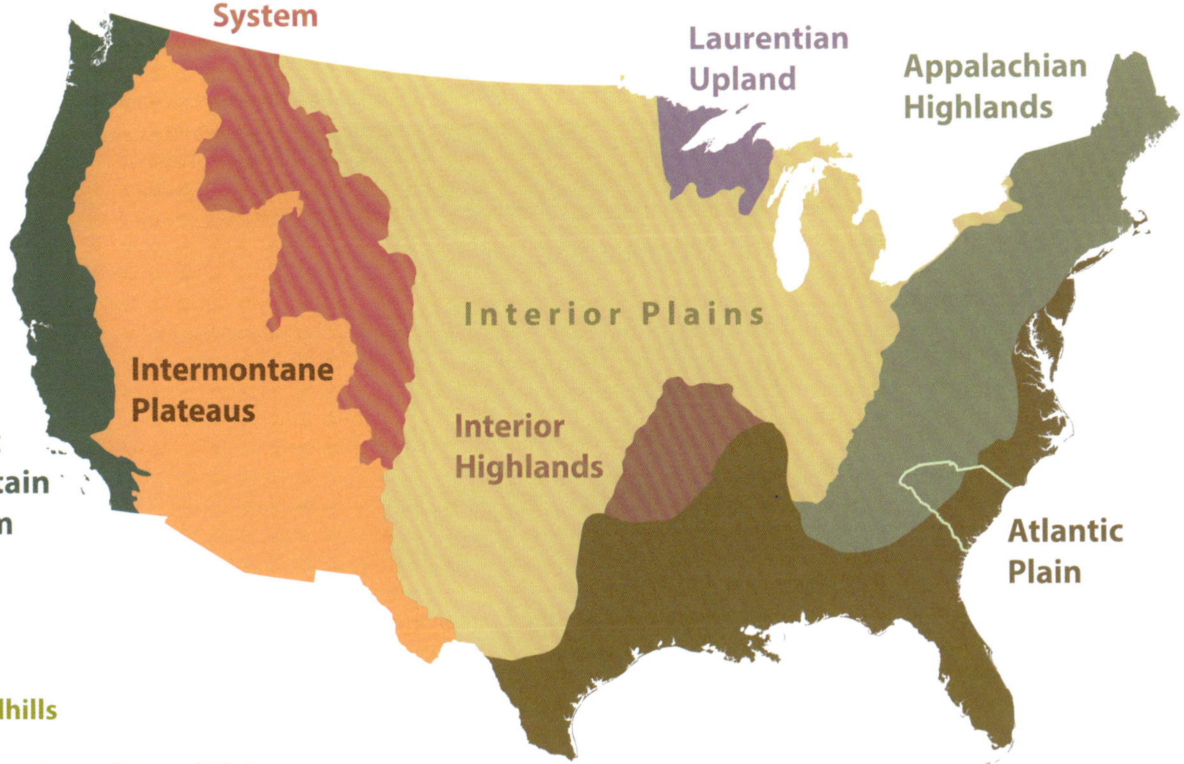

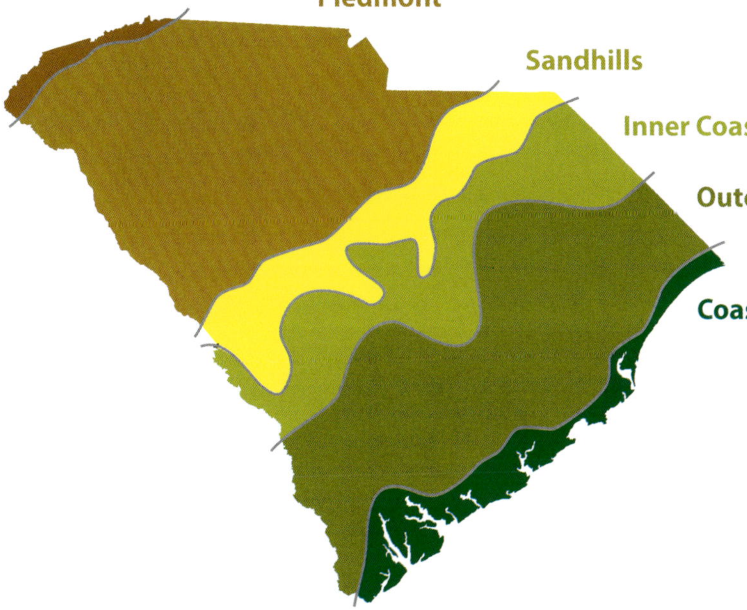

There are six landform regions in South Carolina. The Blue Ridge is mountainous and the Piedmont is rolling and hilly. The Sandhills mark the limit where the ocean once covered much of the state. The Fall Line (shown at right) is located here, where the harder rocks of the Upstate meet the softer rocks of the Lowcountry. The Inner Coastal Plain is hilly, while the Outer Coastal Plain is generally flat. The Coastal Zone contains beaches, islands, and other landform features shaped by the ocean.

EARTHQUAKES

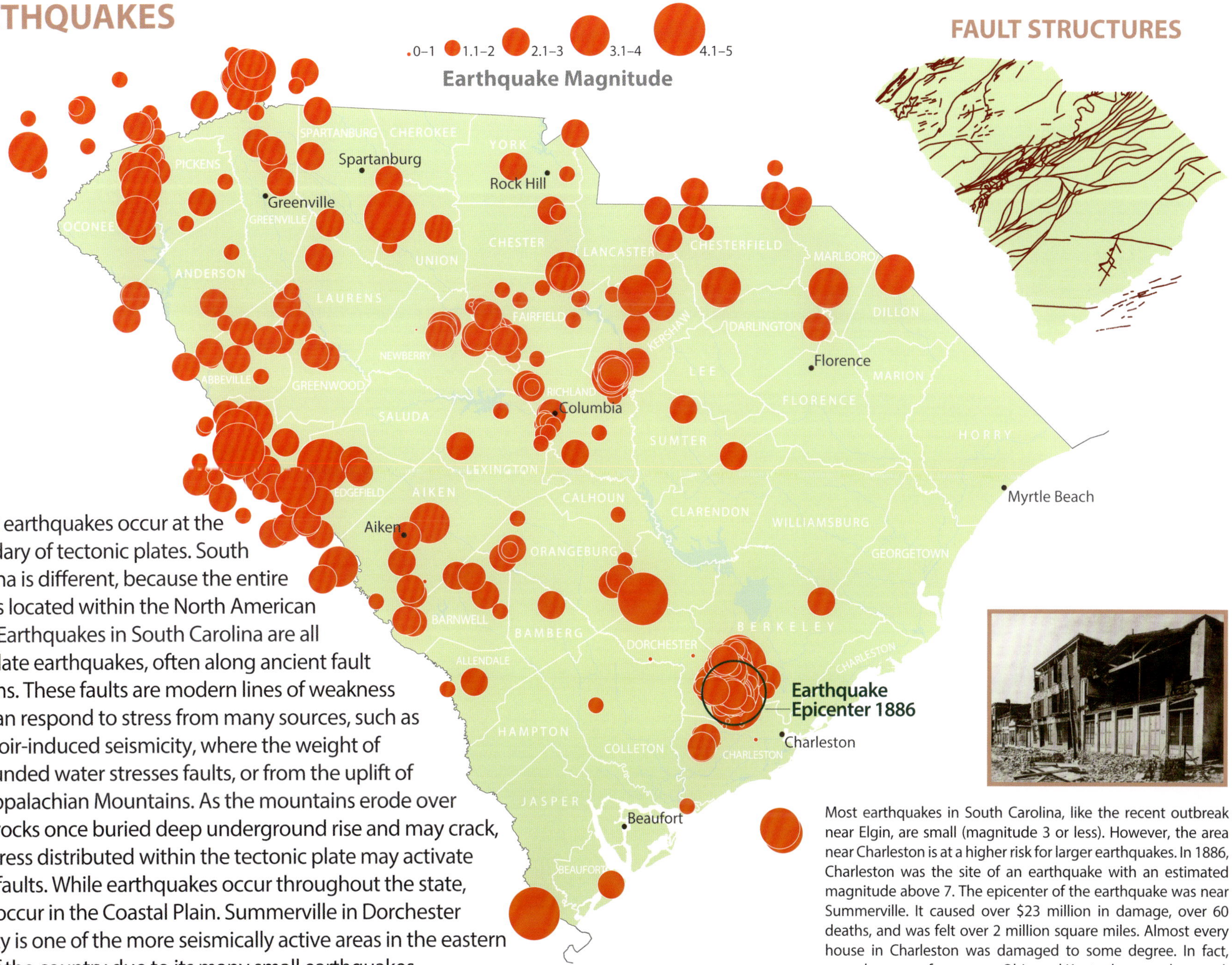

Most earthquakes occur at the boundary of tectonic plates. South Carolina is different, because the entire state is located within the North American Plate. Earthquakes in South Carolina are all intraplate earthquakes, often along ancient fault systems. These faults are modern lines of weakness that can respond to stress from many sources, such as reservoir-induced seismicity, where the weight of impounded water stresses faults, or from the uplift of the Appalachian Mountains. As the mountains erode over time, rocks once buried deep underground rise and may crack, and stress distributed within the tectonic plate may activate older faults. While earthquakes occur throughout the state, most occur in the Coastal Plain. Summerville in Dorchester County is one of the more seismically active areas in the eastern half of the country due to its many small earthquakes.

FAULT STRUCTURES

Most earthquakes in South Carolina, like the recent outbreak near Elgin, are small (magnitude 3 or less). However, the area near Charleston is at a higher risk for larger earthquakes. In 1886, Charleston was the site of an earthquake with an estimated magnitude above 7. The epicenter of the earthquake was near Summerville. It caused over $23 million in damage, over 60 deaths, and was felt over 2 million square miles. Almost every house in Charleston was damaged to some degree. In fact, some homes as far away as Ohio and Kentucky were damaged.

LAND COVER

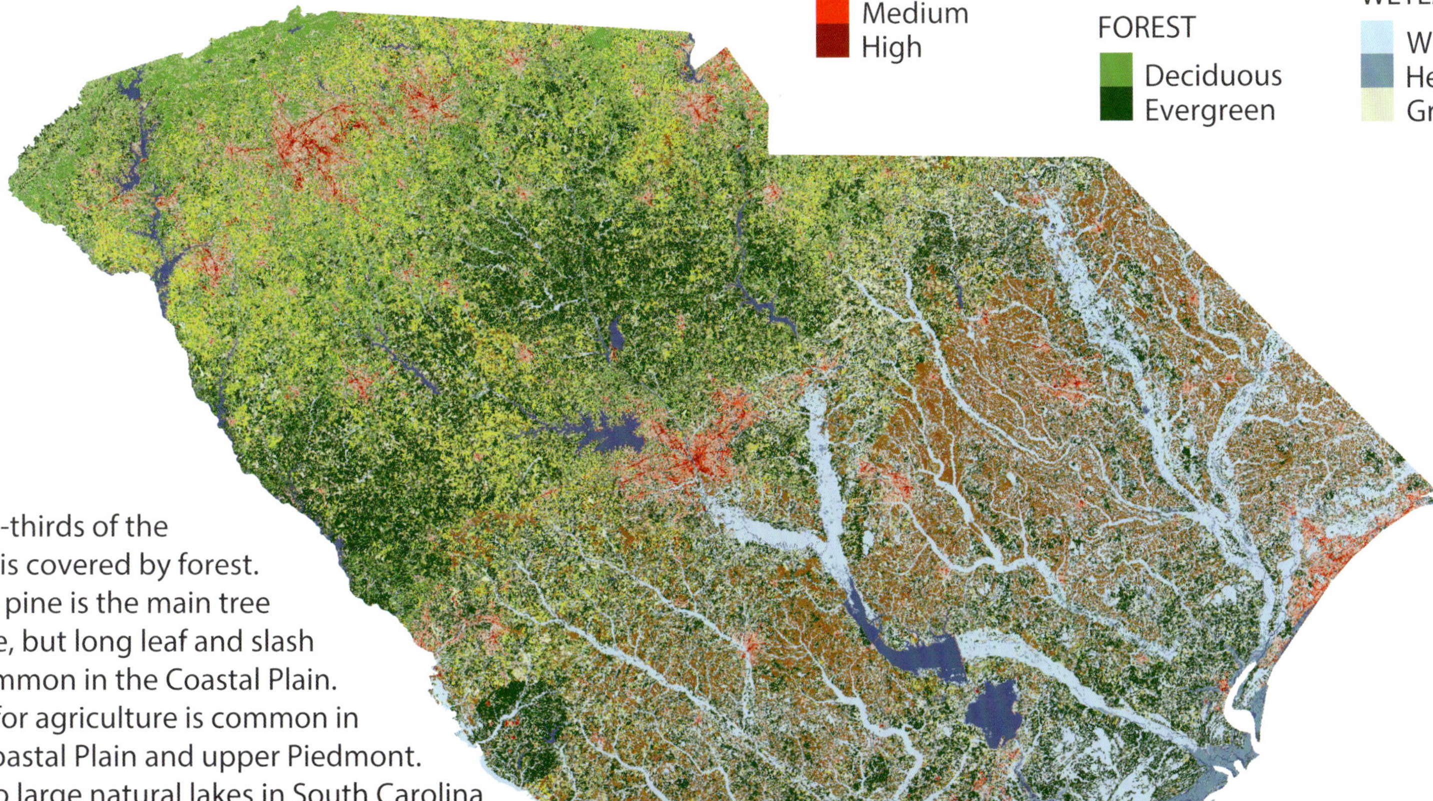

Nearly two-thirds of the state's land is covered by forest. The loblolly pine is the main tree you may see, but long leaf and slash pine are common in the Coastal Plain. Using land for agriculture is common in the Inner Coastal Plain and upper Piedmont. There are no large natural lakes in South Carolina but all major rivers, except the Pee Dee, have dams that created large reservoirs. Wetlands can be found throughout the state but most are located in the Coastal Zone and in the floodplains of major rivers. The spectacular old-growth bottomland hardwood forest found in the Congaree River floodplain includes some of the tallest trees in the eastern United States. South Carolina's urban landscape expanded as its small compact cities began to suburbanize in the 1970s. This urban sprawl is most apparent along the interstate highways that radiate outward from the state's major cities.

The state's large forests have been important resources for its inhabitants. Products like pitch and tar were once used in the shipbuilding industry, while lumber has been used to make homes here for thousands of years. Much of the tree stock harvested today, as seen on this logging truck, is used in the paper industry.

BIODIVERSITY AND CONSERVATION

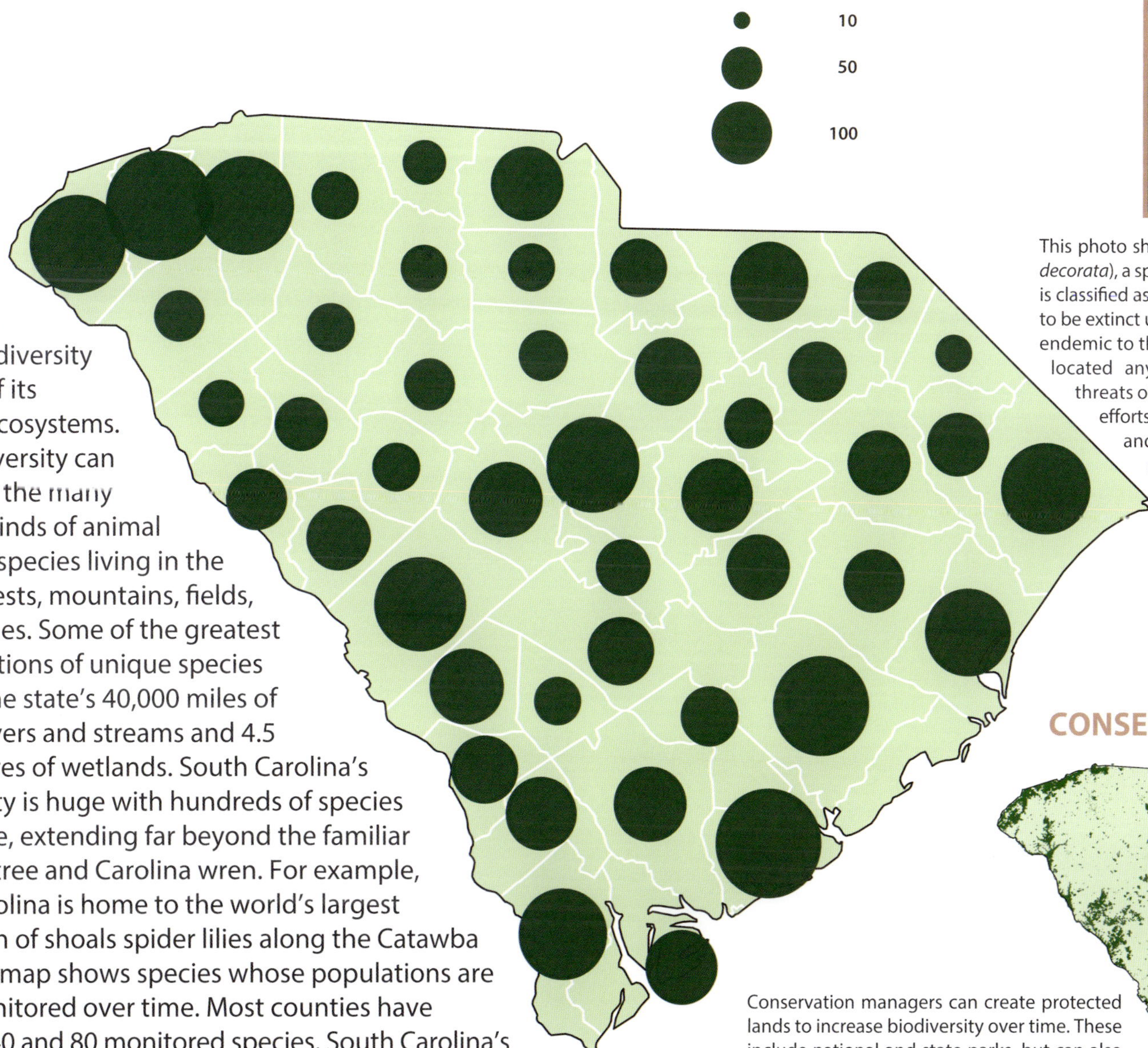

South Carolina is rich in biodiversity because of its different ecosystems. This biodiversity can be seen in the many different kinds of animal and plant species living in the state's forests, mountains, fields, and beaches. Some of the greatest concentrations of unique species occur in the state's 40,000 miles of flowing rivers and streams and 4.5 million acres of wetlands. South Carolina's biodiversity is huge with hundreds of species found here, extending far beyond the familiar palmetto tree and Carolina wren. For example, South Carolina is home to the world's largest population of shoals spider lilies along the Catawba River. The map shows species whose populations are being monitored over time. Most counties have between 40 and 80 monitored species. South Carolina's most recent wildlife action plan lists 493 animals and 332 plants as priority species for conservation monitoring. Many of these species are in decline.

This photo shows the Carolina heelsplitter (*Lasmigona decorata*), a species of mussel found in our waterways. It is classified as an endangered species and was thought to be extinct until it was rediscovered in the 1980s. It is endemic to the Carolinas, meaning this species is not located anywhere else. With few remaining and threats of pollution and habitat loss, conservation efforts are focusing on protecting waterways and attempting to increase their population numbers.

LAND UNDER CONSERVATION PROTECTION

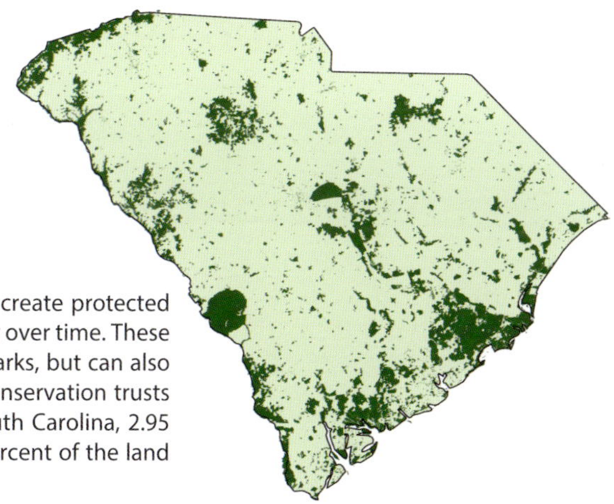

Conservation managers can create protected lands to increase biodiversity over time. These include national and state parks, but can also include land managed by conservation trusts or private individuals. In South Carolina, 2.95 million acres of land (~15 percent of the land area) is protected.

RIVERS, LAKES, AND BAYS

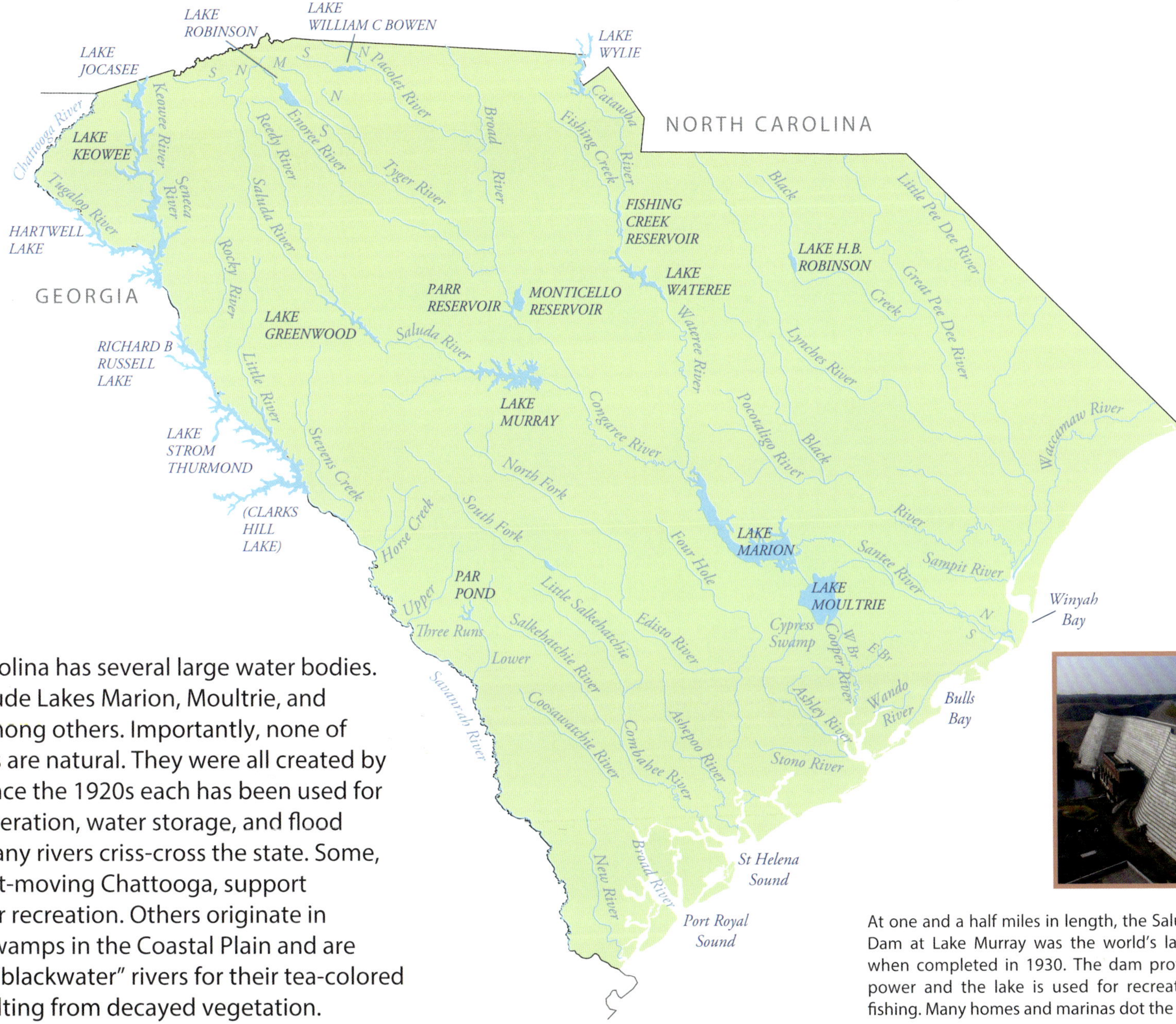

South Carolina has several large water bodies. These include Lakes Marion, Moultrie, and Murray, among others. Importantly, none of these lakes are natural. They were all created by people. Since the 1920s each has been used for power generation, water storage, and flood control. Many rivers criss-cross the state. Some, like the fast-moving Chattooga, support whitewater recreation. Others originate in forested swamps in the Coastal Plain and are known as "blackwater" rivers for their tea-colored water resulting from decayed vegetation.

At one and a half miles in length, the Saluda (Dreher Shoals) Dam at Lake Murray was the world's largest earthen dam when completed in 1930. The dam provides hydroelectric power and the lake is used for recreational boating and fishing. Many homes and marinas dot the lake's shoreline.

CLIMATE REGIONS

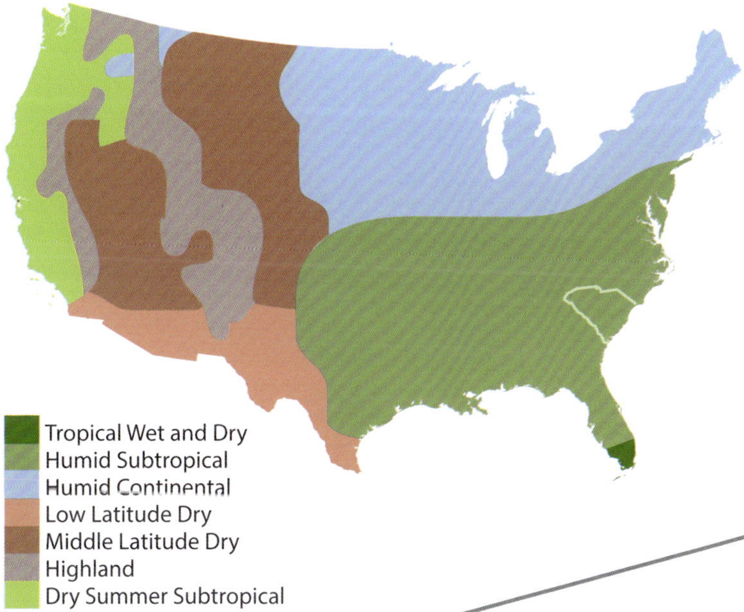

Climate refers to the long-term average weather (precipitation, temperature) of an area. South Carolina is in the Humid Subtropical climate region, which generally has higher temperatures and relative humidity. However, climate controls such as the Blue Ridge Mountains and the Atlantic Ocean create variation across the state. The mountainous Upstate is generally wetter and cooler, while warmer ocean currents moderate winter temperatures in the Lowcountry. Climographs are graphs that show average temperature and precipitation for each month of the year in a specific location.

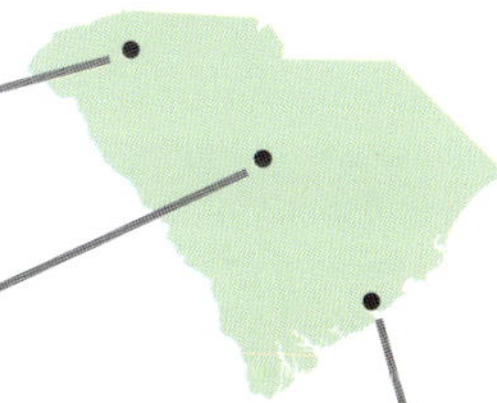

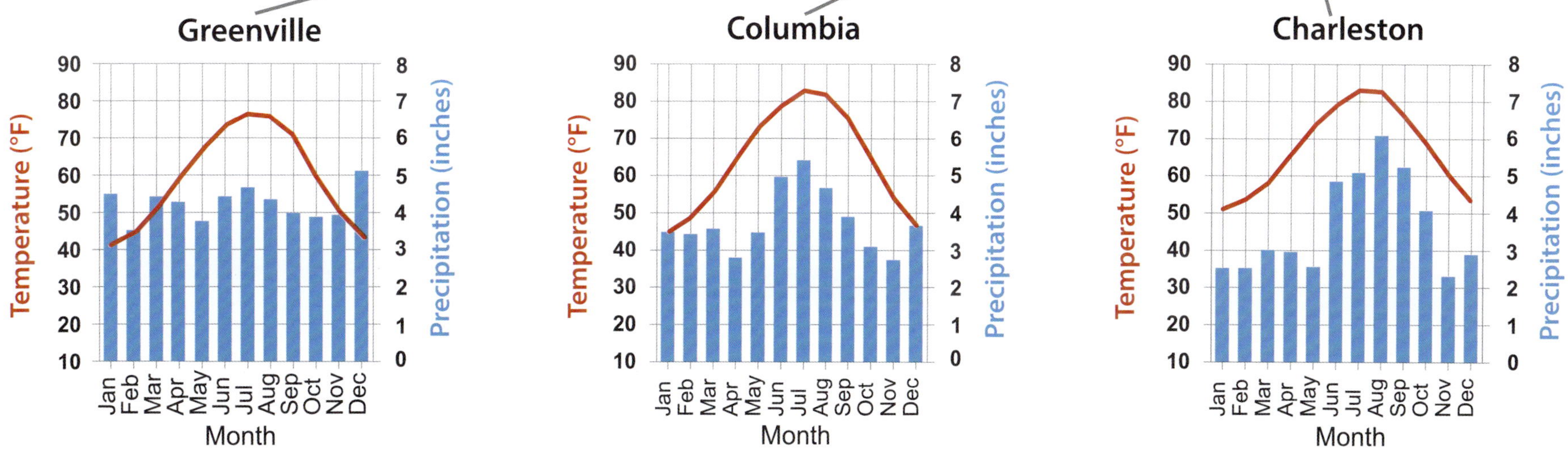

Three climographs, one each from the Piedmont, Midlands, and Coastal Zone, are shown. Variation in precipitation between June and September increases as you move from the Piedmont to the Coastal Zone. The average daily temperature peaks around 80°F for each city during the summer. Similarly, each city has an average daily temperature drop between 41°F and 51°F during the coldest winter months of January and December.

TEMPERATURE AND PRECIPITATION

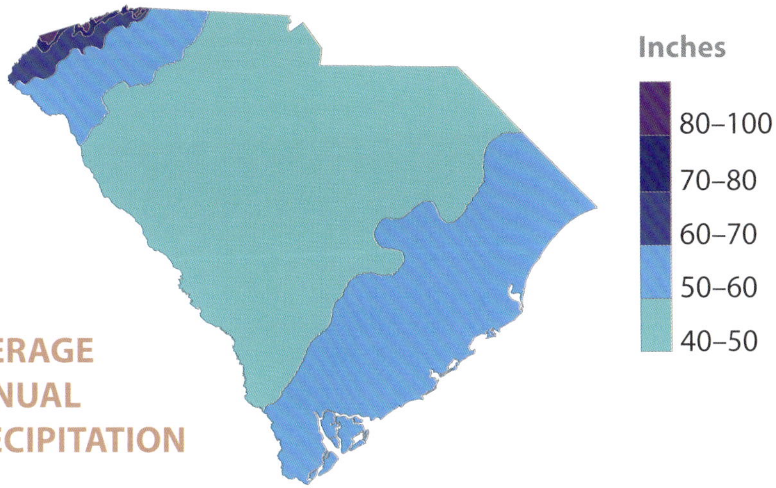

AVERAGE ANNUAL PRECIPITATION

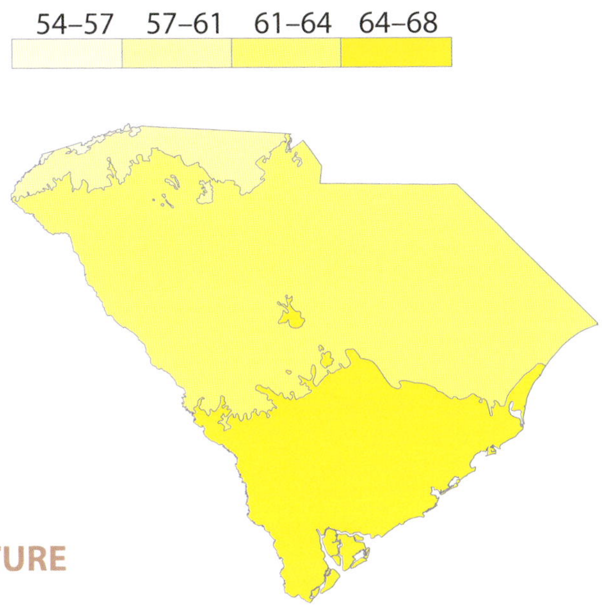

AVERAGE ANNUAL TEMPERATURE

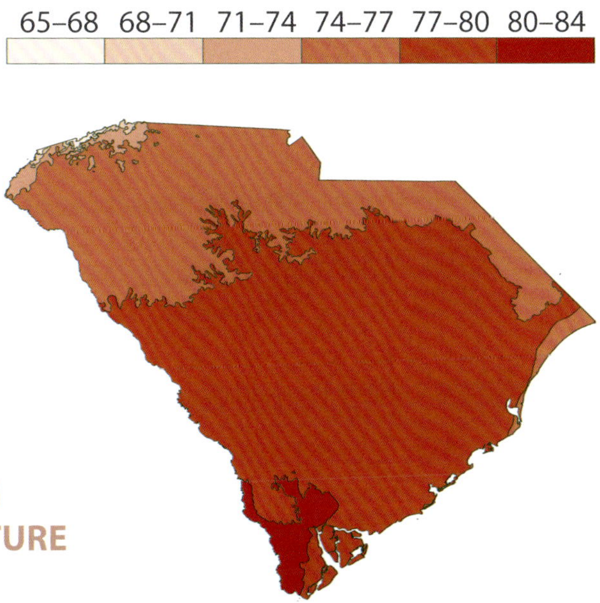

AVERAGE ANNUAL MAXIMUM TEMPERATURE

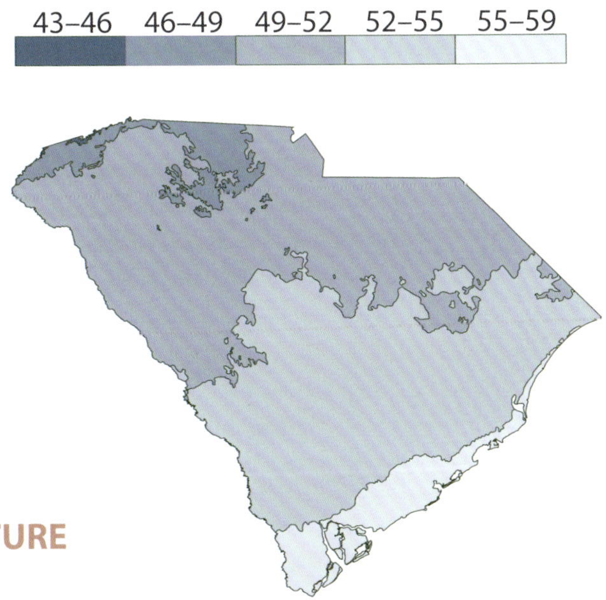

AVERAGE ANNUAL MINIMUM TEMPERATURE

TORNADOES

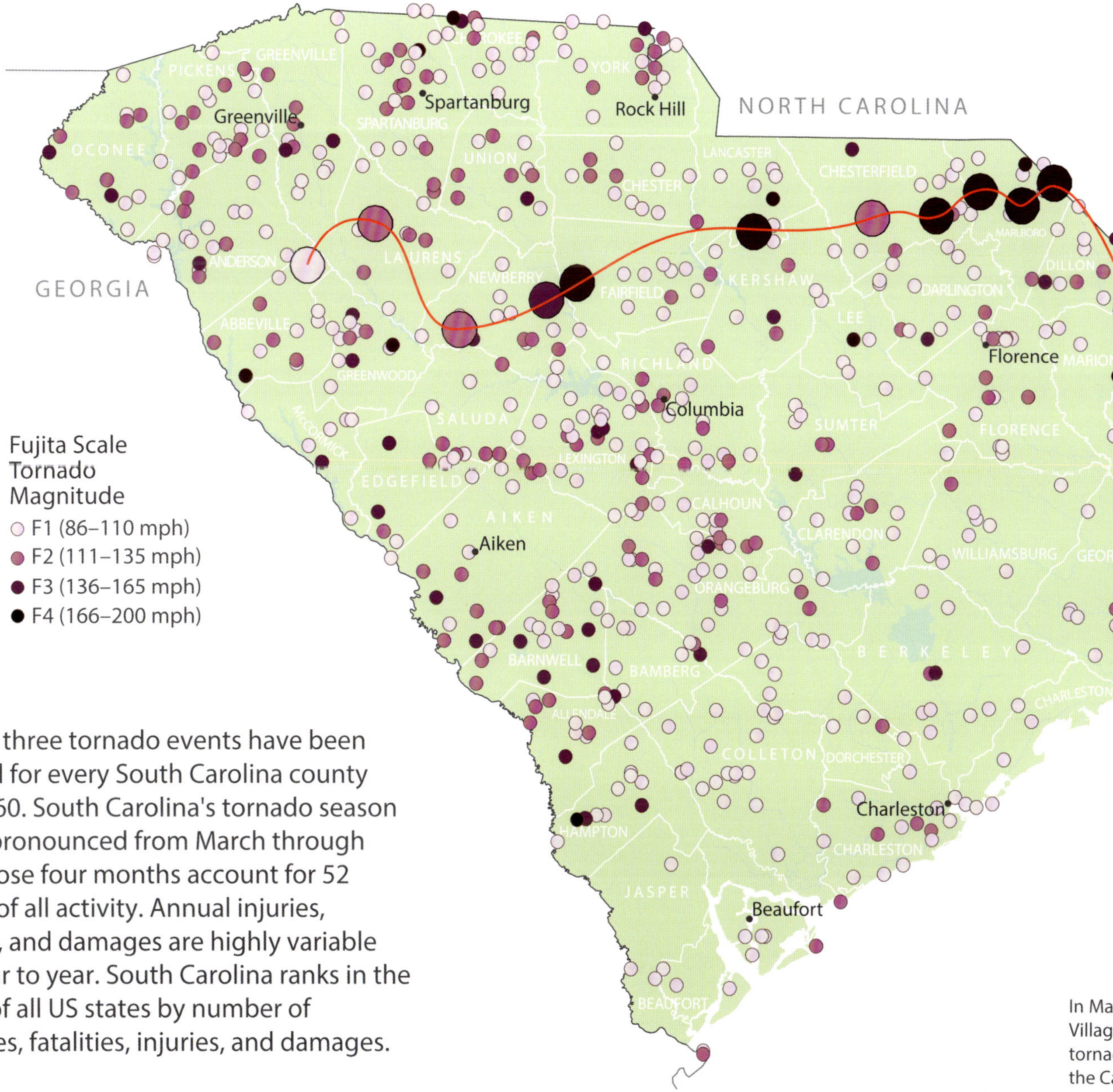

1984 Outbreak

The larger dots and connecting line represent an outbreak of 14 tornadoes in March 1984 resulting in 15 deaths and 448 injuries. The storms stretched from Abbeville and Anderson counties in the west to Marlboro and Horry counties in the east.

At least three tornado events have been recorded for every South Carolina county since 1960. South Carolina's tornado season is most pronounced from March through June. Those four months account for 52 percent of all activity. Annual injuries, fatalities, and damages are highly variable from year to year. South Carolina ranks in the middle of all US states by number of tornadoes, fatalities, injuries, and damages.

In March 1984, a tornado damaged Northwood Village Shopping Plaza in Bennettsville, SC. This tornado was one of a series that swept across the Carolinas during the 1984 outbreak.

HURRICANES

Hurricanes are powerful tropical weather systems that are hundreds of miles across. Winds rotate around a center of low pressure known as the eye. Hurricanes usually develop over warm oceans just north and south of the equator. Hurricanes produce strong winds and large amounts of rain that result in flooding both in coastal and inland areas. The intensity and magnitude of hurricanes is expressed by the Saffir-Simpson Hurricane Scale. This scale is based on wind speed, central pressure, storm surge height, and damage potential. Hurricane Hugo in 1989 was responsible for more than $7 billion dollars in damage to the state. Most hurricanes in the Atlantic Ocean occur between June 1 and November 30. August and September are peak hurricane activity months for South Carolina. As ocean water temperatures rise, warmer waters feed even more energy into tropical weather systems. Hurricanes are becoming more intense and are having worsening impacts like storm surge and rainfall.

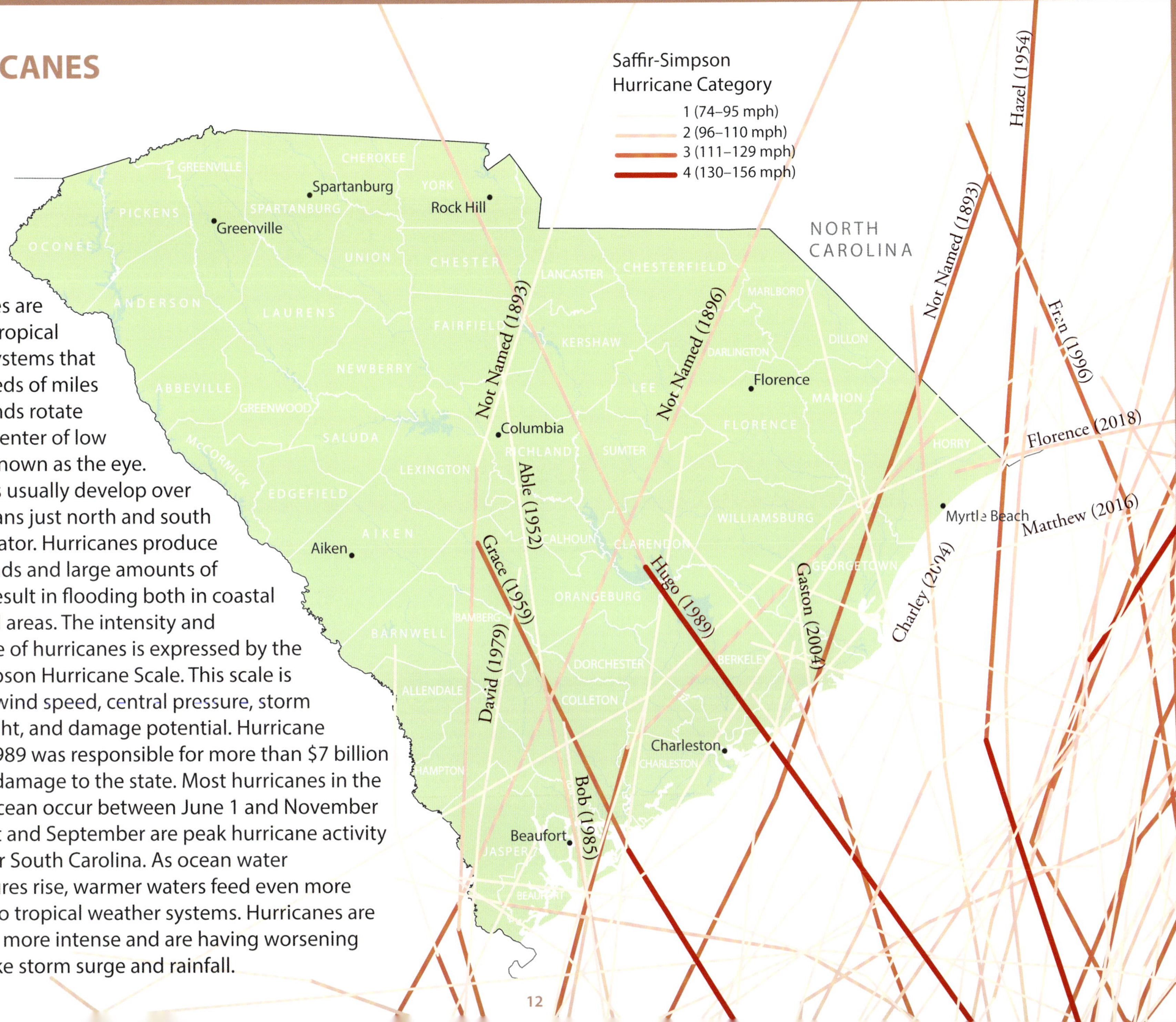

CHANGING ENVIRONMENT

Greenhouse gas pollution is changing South Carolina's environment, including temperature, precipitation and flooding, and sea level rise. Scientists take measurements and use chemistry and physics to understand our changing environment, and communicate their findings through reports and maps. These maps show how temperature is changing in our area over time, which can affect people, plants, and animals. For example, warmer temperatures at night lead to higher energy bills while an extremely hot day can cause illness or make working outdoors unsafe.

INCREASE IN AVERAGE OVERNIGHT LOWS

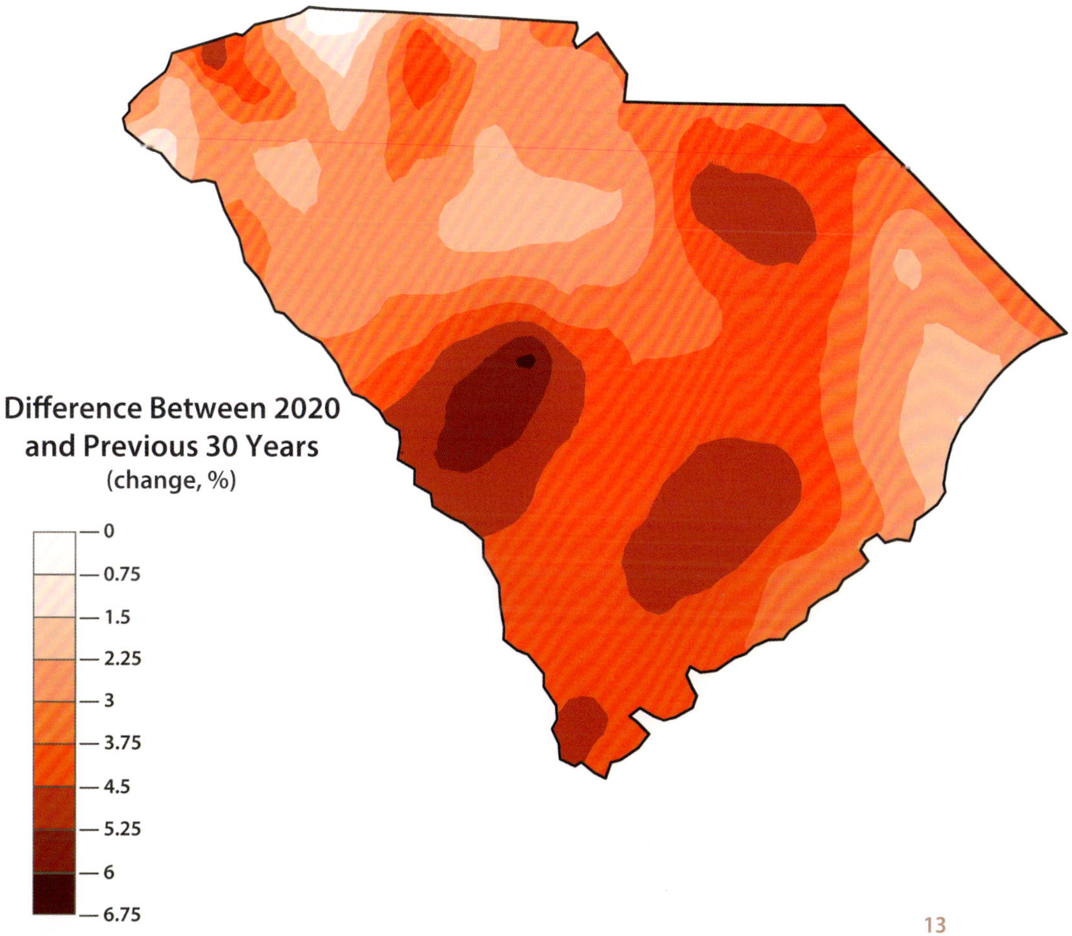

CHANGE IN EXTREMELY HOT DAYS

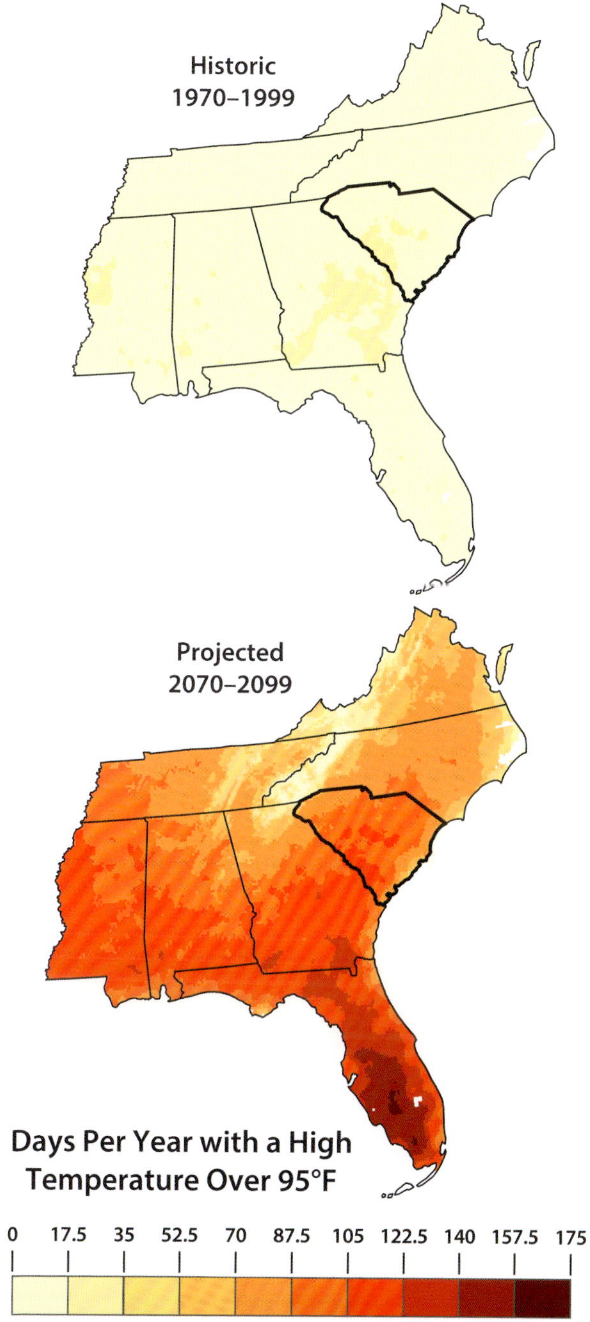

EARLY HUMAN LANDSCAPE

NATIVE AMERICANS, ca. 1670

The state's early human landscape was shaped by peoples migrating from Asia. They arrived in what is now South Carolina about 15,000 to 20,000 years ago, although evidence from an archaeological site in Allendale County may record a much earlier arrival date. When Europeans arrived, there were about 15,000 Native Americans divided into numerous tribes. Their language family was Algonquian, Iroquoian, Muskhogean, Siouan, or Uchean. Their population numbers declined significantly after contact with European settlers due to disease, displacement, and war. Evidence of their subsistence and ceremonial lifestyle is visible today in abandoned shell middens and earthen mounds. Native Americans continue to live in South Carolina today, maintaining a rich legacy in the place names of rivers, counties and towns.

Shell middens and shell rings, made up of pottery shards, bones, and shells, represent the history of early native peoples. These deposits can tell us about their diet and local environment. A shell midden, the Spanish Mount, is easily viewable along a hiking trail at Edisto Beach State Park. The Fig Island shell ring (shown) is located nearby along the North Edisto River.

EUROPEAN CONTACT

A chiefdom refers to a primary village. Cofitachequi, a chiefdom encountered by de Soto and Pardo, is named after the female chieftain, The Lady of Cofitachequi. The Spanish explorers also visited another chiefdom to the northwest —Joara.

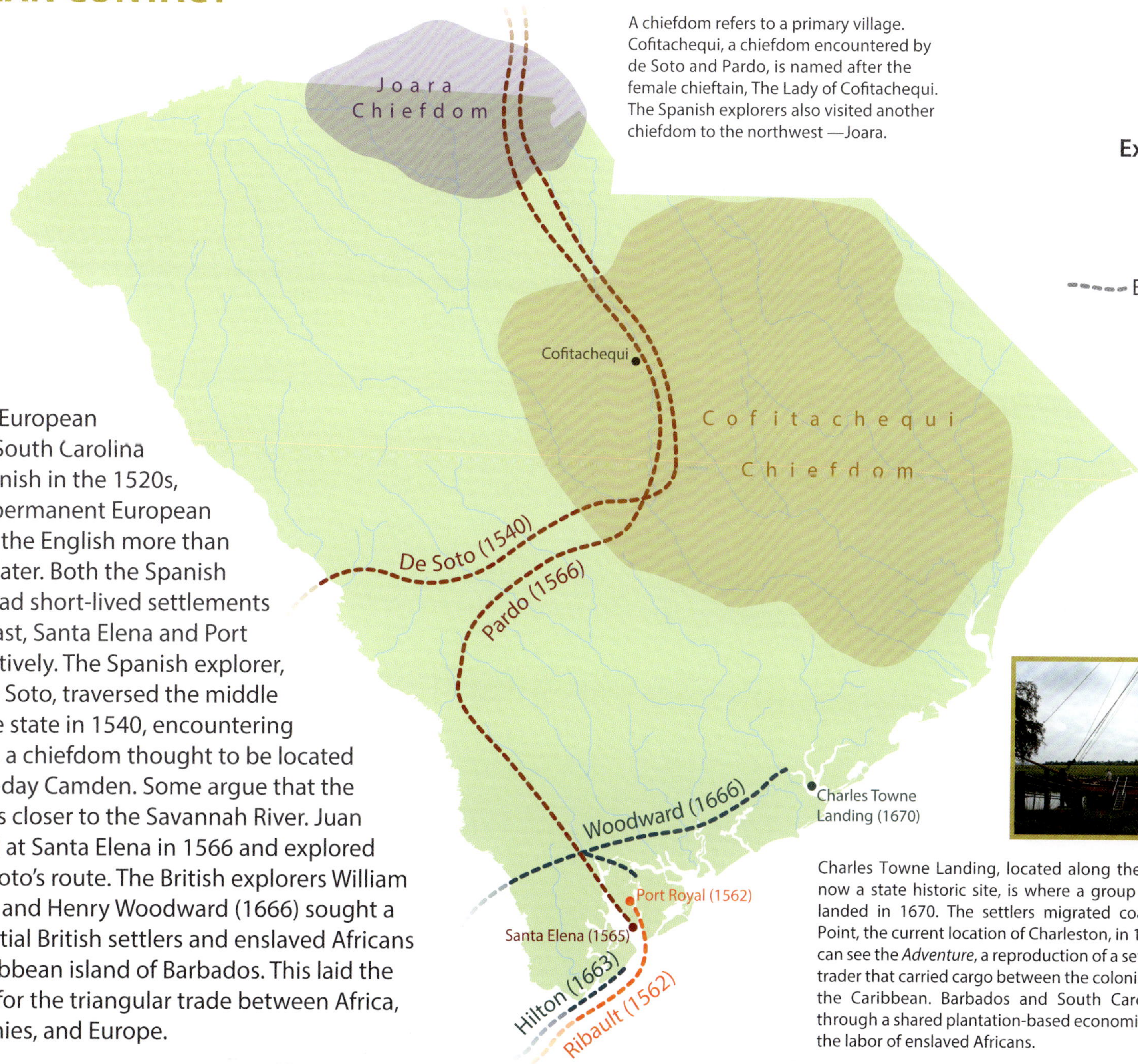

The earliest European explorers of South Carolina were the Spanish in the 1520s, but the first permanent European settlers were the English more than one century later. Both the Spanish and French had short-lived settlements along the coast, Santa Elena and Port Royal, respectively. The Spanish explorer, Hernando de Soto, traversed the middle section of the state in 1540, encountering Cofitachequi, a chiefdom thought to be located near present-day Camden. Some argue that the chiefdom was closer to the Savannah River. Juan Pardo arrived at Santa Elena in 1566 and explored much of de Soto's route. The British explorers William Hilton (1663) and Henry Woodward (1666) sought a site for potential British settlers and enslaved Africans from the Caribbean island of Barbados. This laid the groundwork for the triangular trade between Africa, Britain's colonies, and Europe.

Charles Towne Landing, located along the Ashley River and now a state historic site, is where a group of English settlers landed in 1670. The settlers migrated coastward to Oyster Point, the current location of Charleston, in 1680. Visitors today can see the *Adventure*, a reproduction of a seventeenth-century trader that carried cargo between the colonies and Barbados in the Caribbean. Barbados and South Carolina were linked through a shared plantation-based economic system reliant on the labor of enslaved Africans.

COLONIAL LANDSCAPE

GENERALIZED PATTERNS OF COLONIAL AGRICULTURE

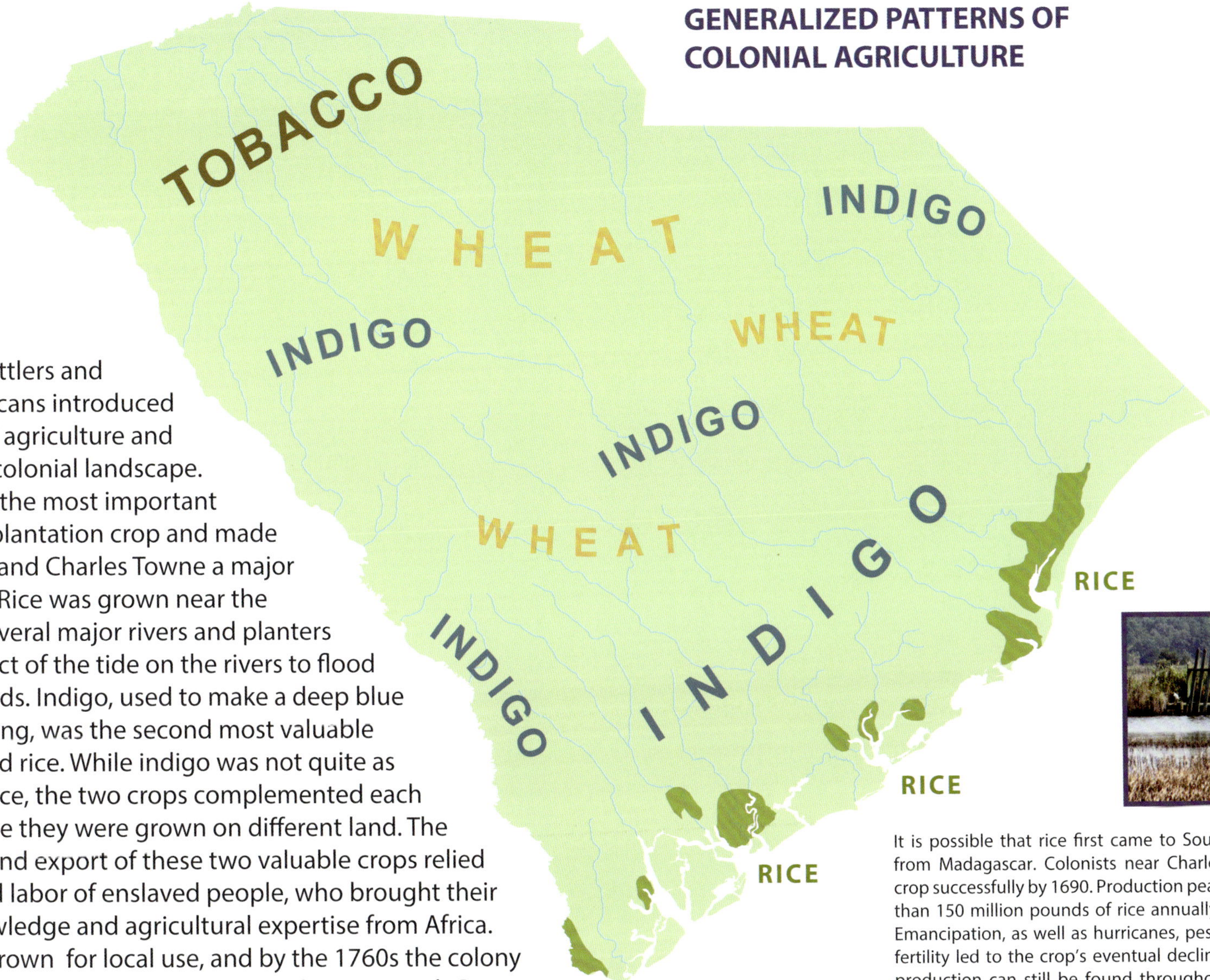

European settlers and enslaved Africans introduced new forms of agriculture and crops to the colonial landscape. Rice became the most important commercial plantation crop and made planters rich and Charles Towne a major colonial city. Rice was grown near the mouths of several major rivers and planters used the effect of the tide on the rivers to flood and drain fields. Indigo, used to make a deep blue dye for clothing, was the second most valuable export behind rice. While indigo was not quite as valuable as rice, the two crops complemented each other because they were grown on different land. The production and export of these two valuable crops relied on the forced labor of enslaved people, who brought their cultural knowledge and agricultural expertise from Africa. Wheat was grown for local use, and by the 1760s the colony was exporting flour to the Caribbean. Tobacco, a Back Country crop, was harder to sell because it was far from Charles Towne.

It is possible that rice first came to South Carolina in 1685 from Madagascar. Colonists near Charles Towne grew the crop successfully by 1690. Production peaked in 1850 at more than 150 million pounds of rice annually. The Civil War and Emancipation, as well as hurricanes, pests, and reduced soil fertility led to the crop's eventual decline. Remnants of rice production can still be found throughout the Lowcountry. Pictured here are rice trunks used to manage the flow of tidal waters in and out of rice fields.

TOWNSHIP SYSTEM, 1731–1765

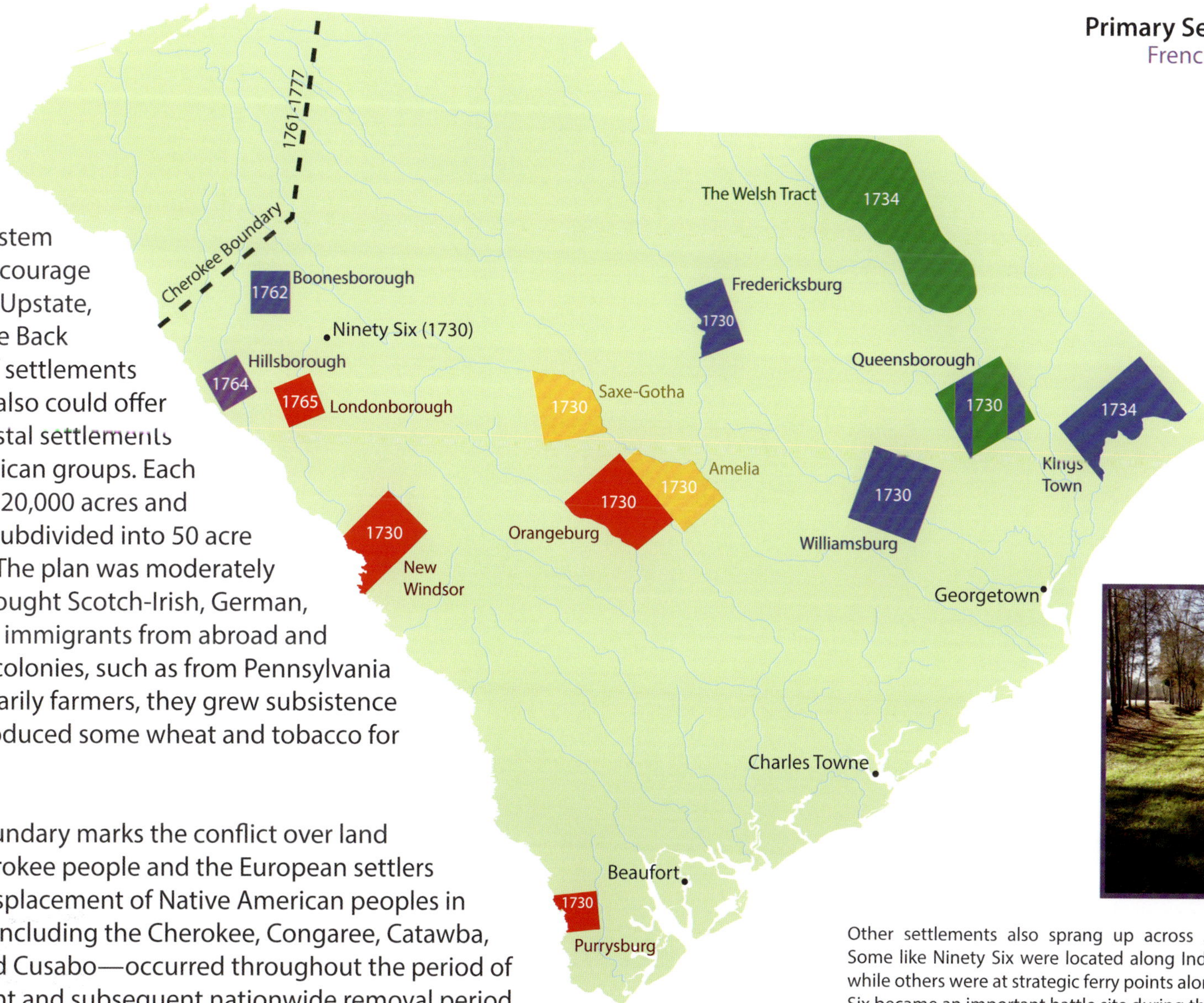

The Township System was created to encourage settlement in the Upstate, known then as the Back Country. A ring of settlements in the hinterland also could offer protection to coastal settlements from Native American groups. Each town was at least 20,000 acres and could be further subdivided into 50 acre household plots. The plan was moderately successful and brought Scotch-Irish, German, Swiss, and French immigrants from abroad and elsewhere in the colonies, such as from Pennsylvania and Virginia. Primarily farmers, they grew subsistence crops but also produced some wheat and tobacco for cash sale.

The Cherokee Boundary marks the conflict over land between the Cherokee people and the European settlers in the Upstate. Displacement of Native American peoples in South Carolina—including the Cherokee, Congaree, Catawba, Creek, Siouan, and Cusabo—occurred throughout the period of colonial settlement and subsequent nationwide removal period of the 1800s. After the Cherokee lost their land in South Carolina, they were later forced to march the Trail of Tears.

Other settlements also sprang up across South Carolina. Some like Ninety Six were located along Indian trade paths while others were at strategic ferry points along rivers. Ninety Six became an important battle site during the Revolutionary War, changing hands between Continentals and Loyalists. The traces of several colonial-era roads are still visible in the landscape as shown here.

COLONIAL ROADS AND REVOLUTIONARY WAR ENGAGEMENTS

COLONIAL ROADS, ca. 1770–1780

South Carolina's population reached about 180,000 before the Revolutionary War. As more people settled the Back Country and planted tradable crops like tobacco and wheat, trading centers such as Camden, Ninety Six, Cheraw, and Congaree emerged in the interior. A series of roads was developed to connect these places together and to Charles Towne. Rivers were also important means for moving goods.

The Revolutionary War caused upheaval in the Colonial period. South Carolina had more battles and military encounters than any other colony, but the major battles of the Revolutionary War took place in the northern colonies. Battles at Camden, Kings Mountain, and Cowpens were important to the outcome of the war.

REVOLUTIONARY WAR ENGAGEMENTS

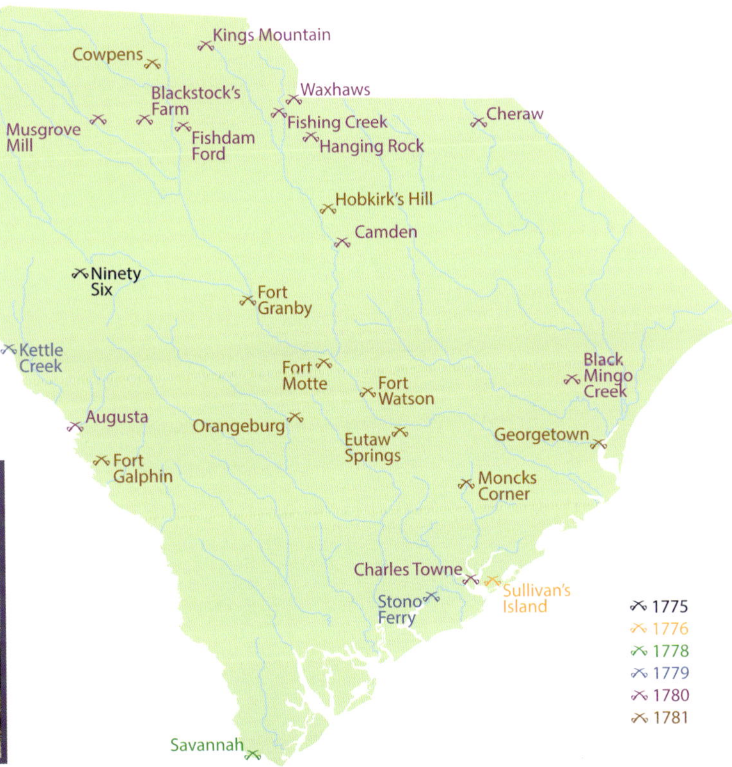

Dozens of Revolutionary War battles of various sizes occurred in South Carolina. Among these was the Battle of Hobkirk's Hill in the Camden area. Surrounded today by homes, the battlefield was the site of a British victory in 1781 over a small army commanded by Nathanael Greene. Re-enactors in British military attire are shown here at the site.

5 ANTEBELLUM LANDSCAPE

POPULATION CHANGE, 1800–1830

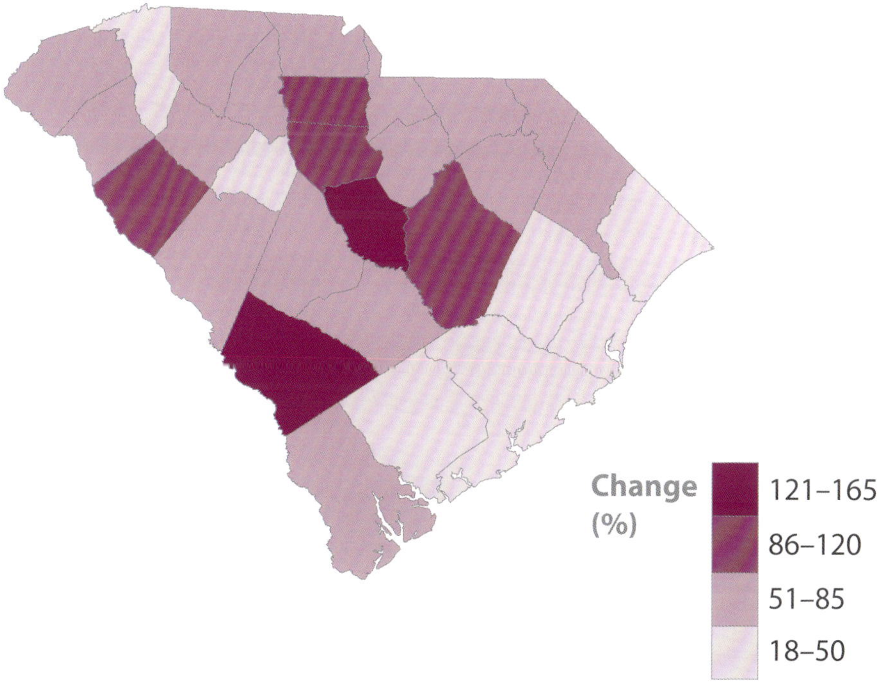

South Carolina's population more than doubled during the antebellum period. This growth varied considerably over time, from place to place, and in racial composition. Between 1800 and 1830, the total population grew by about 68 percent with the highest growth rate occurring in the interior. Growth was much slower during the latter part of the antebellum period due to a stagnating economy. Few immigrants came to South Carolina and there was a strong outmigration of planters, farmers, and enslaved people. Many people left to find more fertile soils or cheaper land in Georgia, Alabama, and Mississippi.

The economy and landscape of South Carolina changed dramatically after the Revolution. Rice was still important in the Lowcountry, but indigo and tobacco were replaced by cotton in the Back Country as the main plantation crop. Cotton spread quickly because of the high demand from England's textile industry, the invention of the cotton gin, better transportation links like canals and railroads, and the merchant class in Charleston. More people, both free and enslaved, came to live in South Carolina as the plantation economy grew.

POPULATION CHANGE, 1830–1860

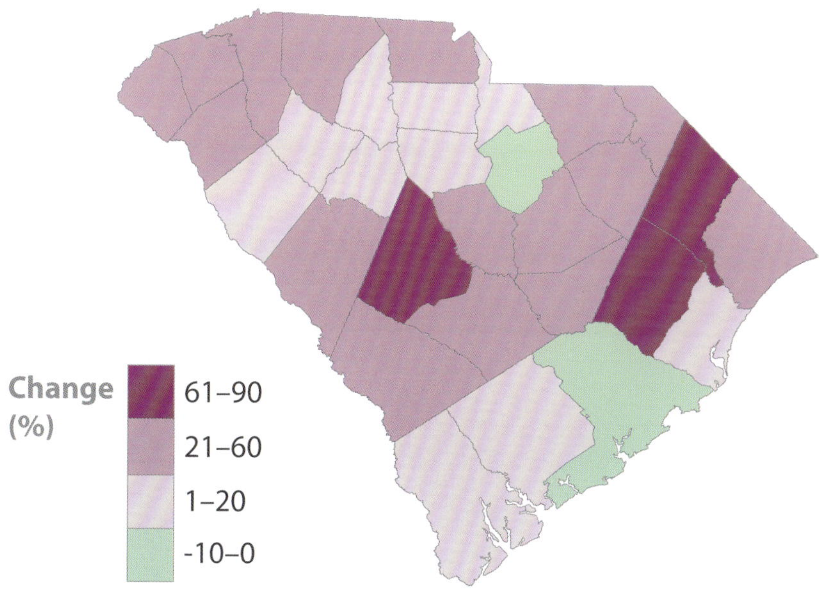

AGRICULTURE AND INDUSTRY, ca. 1840

AGRICULTURE

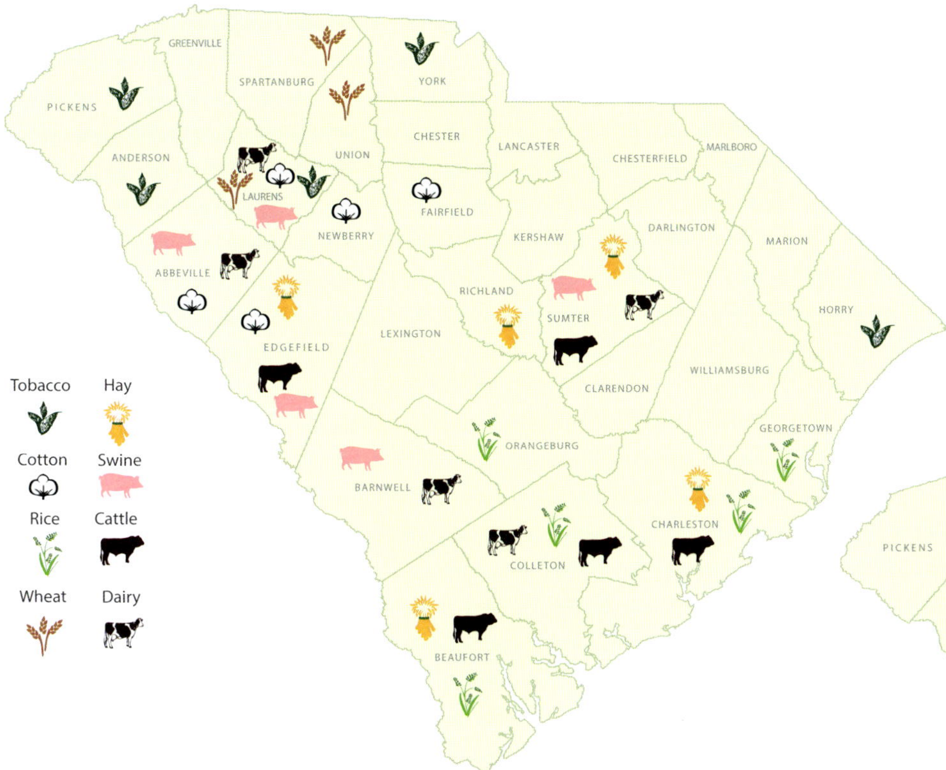

South Carolina's antebellum economy was dominated by agriculture. Rice, tobacco, and cotton were the main crops, but farms also produced wheat, hay, vegetables and fruits, dairy products, cattle, and swine.

Brick manufacturing occurred throughout South Carolina, often as a small-scale activity on plantations. Larger industrial operations began to appear during the nineteenth century. An example from later in that period is the Guignard Brick Works near Columbia where the remnants of beehive kilns are still present. The kilns are now surrounded by apartment homes near the riverfront walkway along the Congaree River.

Manufacturing of textiles and associated mill villages emerged after 1830. Before this there was little manufacturing except for a few flour and saw mills. Railroads helped to sell South Carolina's goods, but also brought competition from other states. Small-scale iron-making occurred in the Upstate, but it struggled against superior products made in northern foundries. Gold deposits were worked in Lancaster, Spartanburg, and Union counties. The map shows the leading areas for some of these products.

INDUSTRY AND MINING

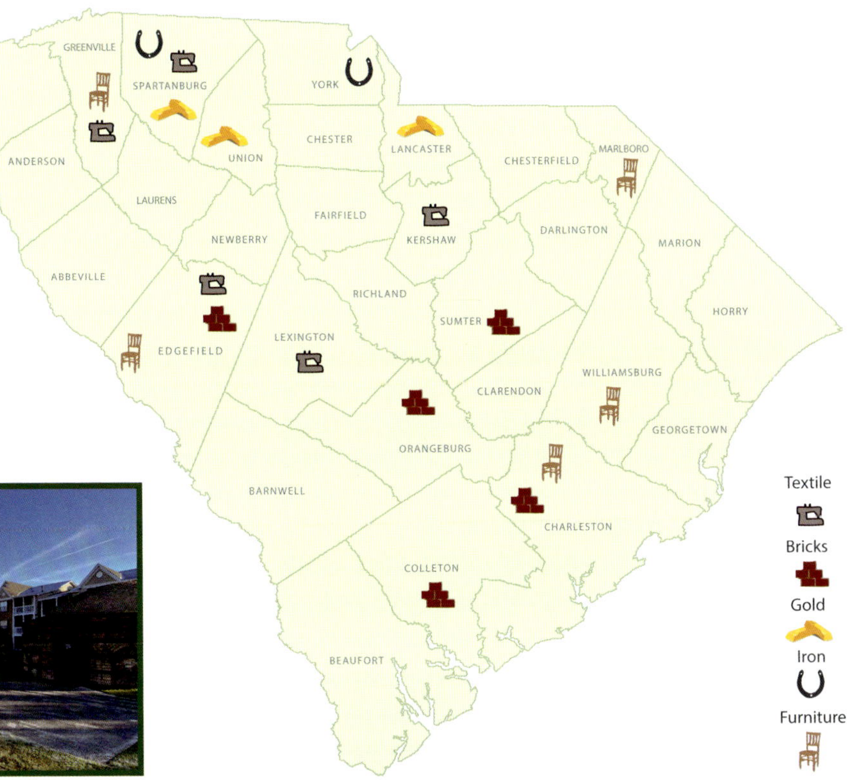

SLAVERY

YEAR IN WHICH ENSLAVED POPULATION FIRST EXCEEDED 50 PERCENT

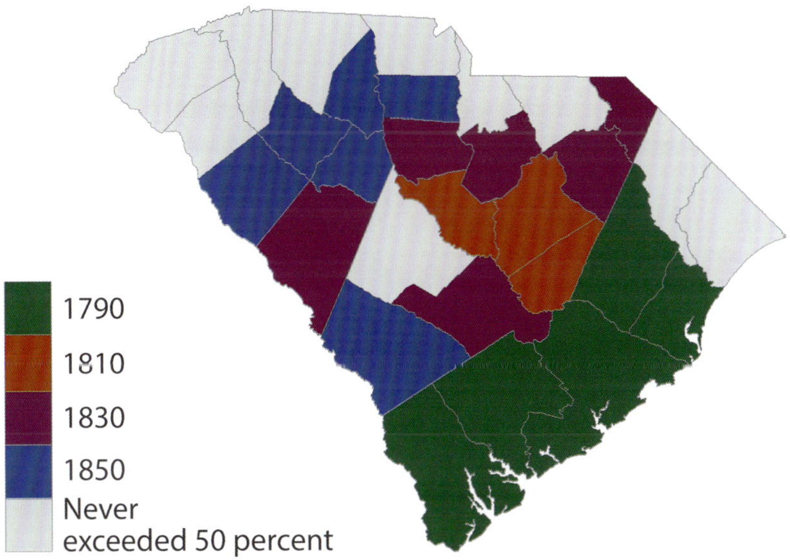

Some early English colonists from Barbados brought enslaved Africans to South Carolina, where they established commercial plantation agriculture. South Carolina's main crop, rice, was very labor intensive. This demand for labor fueled the slave trade. The port of Charleston quickly became the hub and largest site of the slave trade in colonial America. By 1730, Blacks outnumbered Whites two to one in the Lowcountry, the main area of the plantation economy and enslaved population during the colonial period. In the antebellum period, upland cotton expanded the enslaved population to the Back Country.

Enslaved people from West Africa were valued for their rice cultivation skills. They knew how to clear river floodplains, build dikes to create fields, and use the ebb and flow of the tide for irrigation. They also brought diverse music, food, and folk craft traditions from different African regions to South Carolina's culture. Gullah, a creole language that combines West African languages and English, is a unique part of South Carolina's coastal geography. The language is still spoken today in the Sea Islands and coastal areas stretching from North Carolina to Florida.

ENSLAVED, 1860

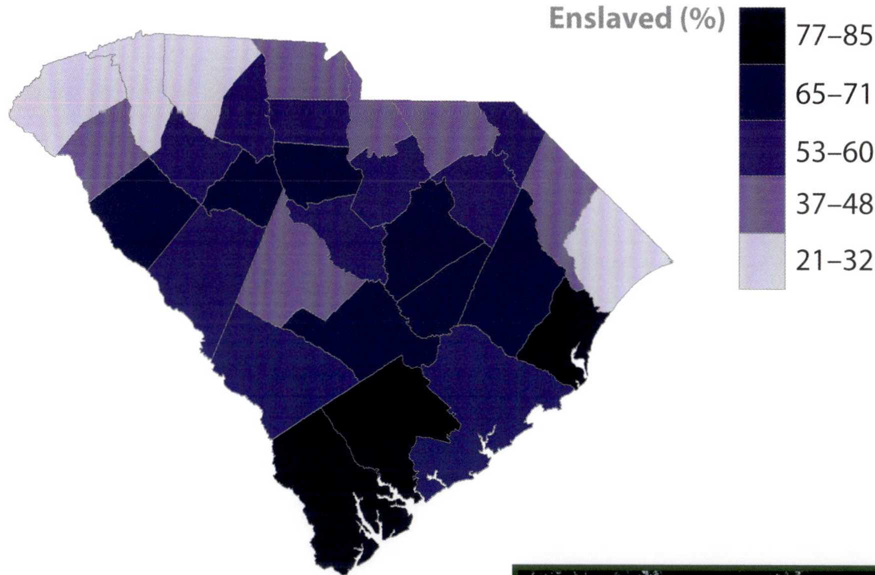

One way that the legacy of slavery is still evident in South Carolina's landscape is in the form of slave quarters. These small dwellings, often in rows, were separate from the main plantation house. They were usually made from wood, about 15 by 20 feet in area, with simple windows and a door. Brick piers raised them off the ground.

Gullah Geechee Communities in Coastal South Carolina

South Carolina's cultural traditions have been influenced by the legacies of enslaved Africans who were forcibly brought to the state to work on rice, indigo, and cotton plantations. Some who escaped the violence of slavery found refuge in South Carolina's Sea Islands and remote interior places. The Gullah Geechee people, many of whom are descendents of enslaved West Africans, have developed and retained unique culinary, artistic, and linguistic practices that blend African, European, and Native American traditions. For example, Gullah is a unique language developed and spoken by Gullah Geechee communities, and their praise songs have influenced musical genres like jazz. Their rural and isolated location around South Carolina's Sea Islands helped to cultivate and maintain these cultural practices. Gullah Geechee communities continue to live in the state's coastal areas, though many are threatened by expanding development of neighborhoods and tourism.

Hoppin' John is a dish of rice, bacon, peas, onions, and spices. Likely a blend of West African and French food traditions, enslaved people brought this recipe from the Caribbean to the Carolinas where it remains an important regional dish. It is seen as good luck to eat a bowl on New Year's Day.

Sea grass basketry is a folk art tradition in the state that blends cultural practices from West Africa, Europe, and Indigenous peoples. Sweetgrass baskets, seen here for sale in Mt. Pleasant, are the official state craft of South Carolina. Development along Highway 17 brings more traffic to vendors but also threatens to displace Gullah artists and limit availability of sea grasses.

The Penn School was the first school in the South for formerly enslaved African Americans. In order to learn skills like carpentry and interior design, students were tasked with building cottages on campus. Gantt Cottage, pictured here, was used by Martin Luther King, Jr. as a retreat between 1964–1967.

During slavery, praise houses were places where enslaved people could worship independently. After emancipation, these small buildings remained important sites for community meetings and worship, which often included singing, clapping, and shouts bridging Christian practices with those of African religions.

CANALS AND RAILROADS

CANALS, ca. 1825

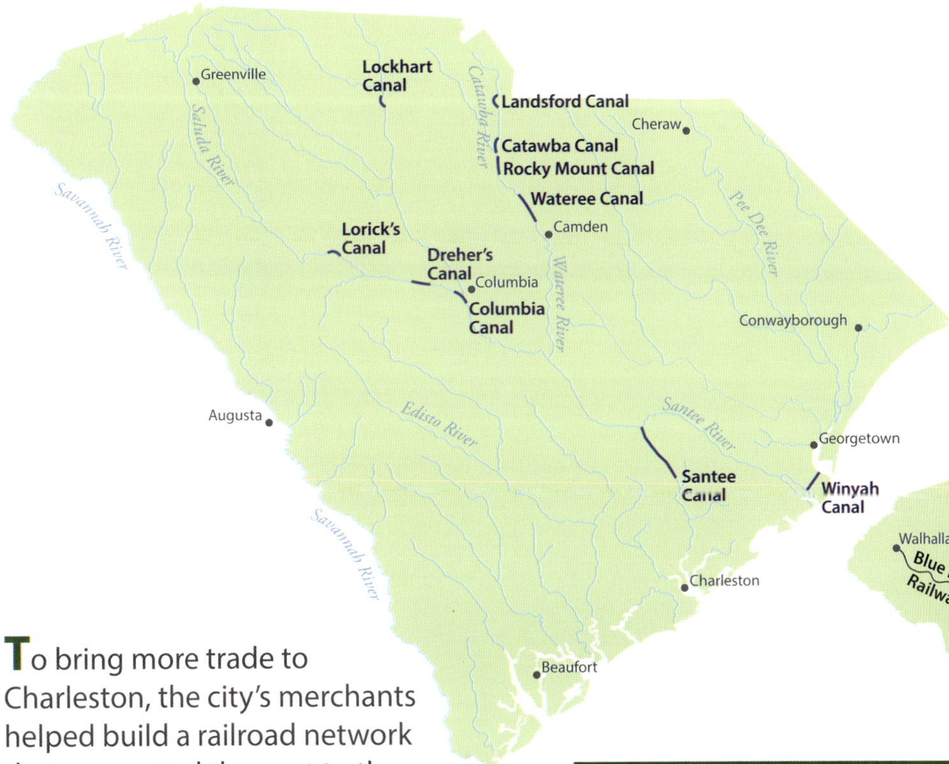

The economic success of upland cotton plantations depended on the efficient transport of cotton from the Back Country to Charleston and then on to markets abroad. Canal systems were an important transportation project that supported these economic connections. The Santee Canal, financed by merchants in the 1790s, and a series of short canals financed by the state in the 1820s, bypassed rapids and expanded the navigability of the river system.

RAILROADS, ca. 1860

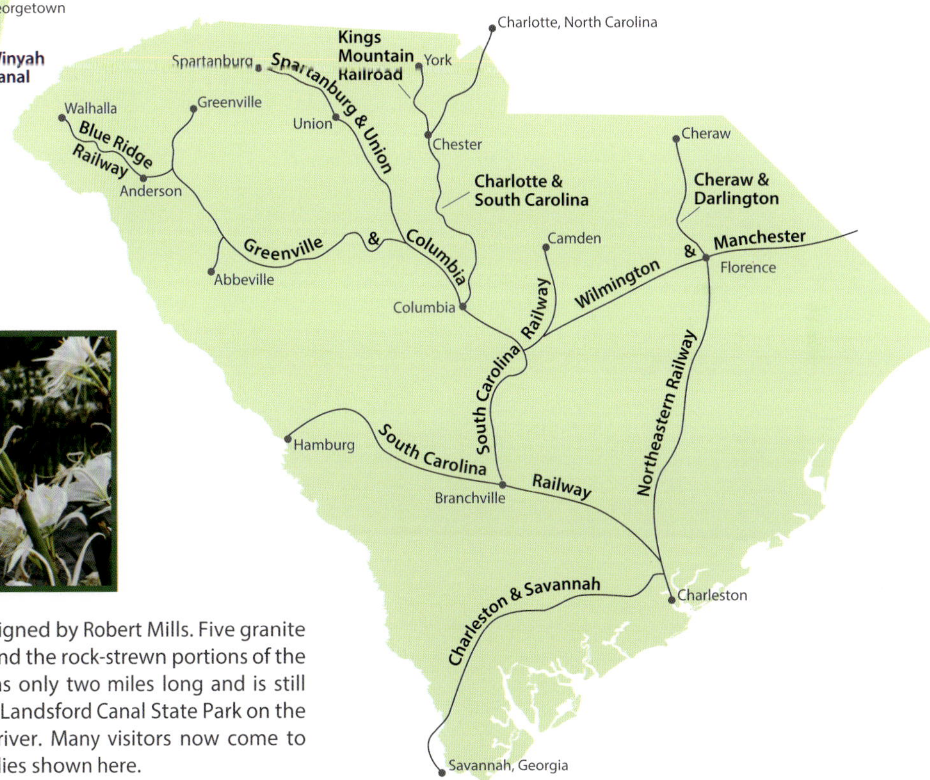

To bring more trade to Charleston, the city's merchants helped build a railroad network that connected the port to the Savannah River and other regions of the state. The first railroad captured cotton shipments on the Savannah River and ran from Charleston to Hamburg, beginning operation in 1834. Connections to the Upstate came later via Columbia. The rail pattern at the end of the antebellum period resembled a river system with trade flowing from all corners of the state to Charleston.

The Landsford Canal was designed by Robert Mills. Five granite locks moved river traffic around the rock-strewn portions of the Catawba River. The canal was only two miles long and is still visible along a hiking path at Landsford Canal State Park on the Chester County side of the river. Many visitors now come to view the rocky shoal spider lilies shown here.

CIVIL WAR

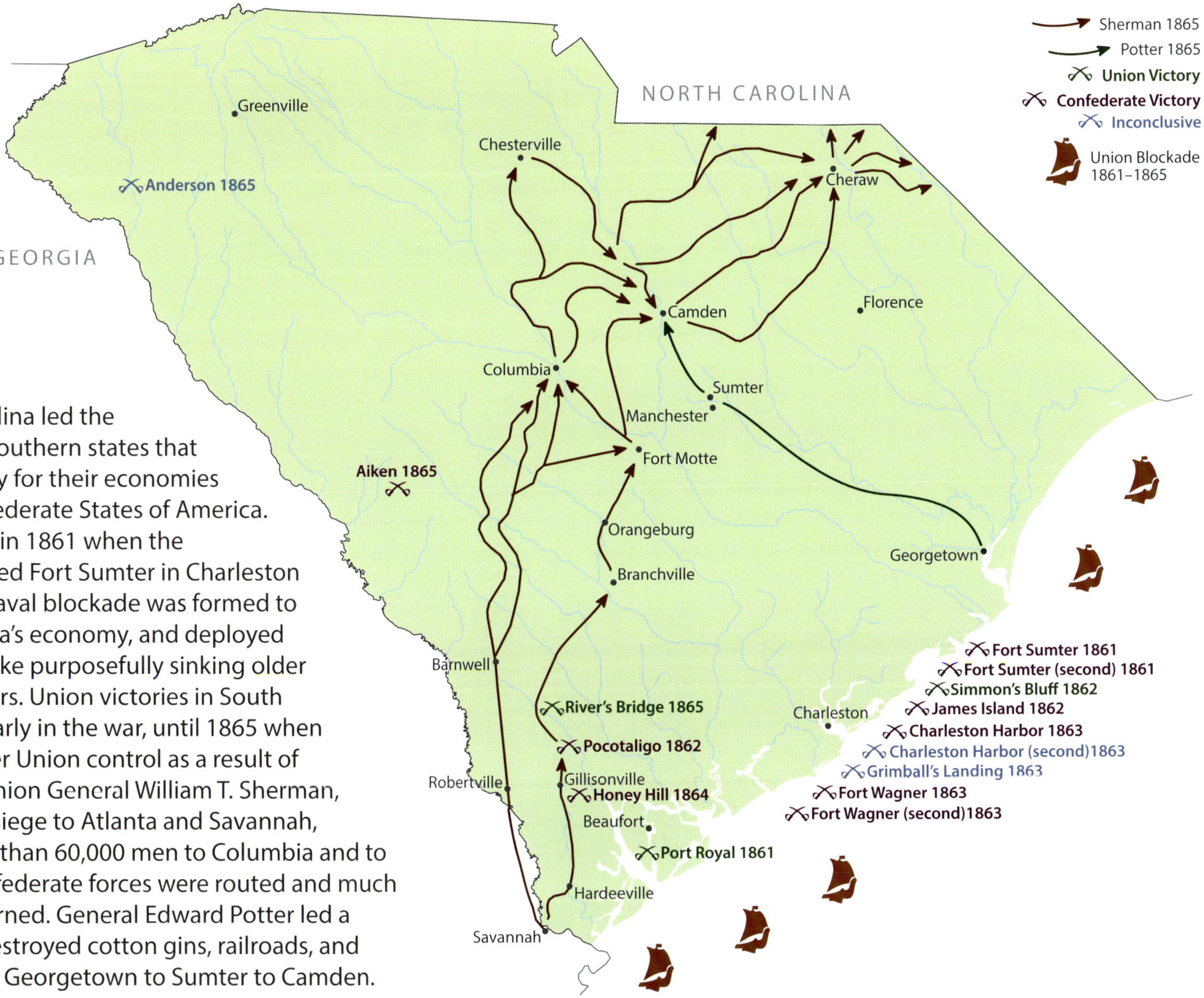

In 1860, South Carolina led the secession of seven southern states that depended on slavery for their economies in forming the Confederate States of America. The Civil War began in 1861 when the Confederates attacked Fort Sumter in Charleston harbor. The Union naval blockade was formed to choke South Carolina's economy, and deployed wartime strategies like purposefully sinking older ships to block harbors. Union victories in South Carolina were few early in the war, until 1865 when the state came under Union control as a result of Sherman's March. Union General William T. Sherman, already having laid siege to Atlanta and Savannah, marched with more than 60,000 men to Columbia and to North Carolina. Confederate forces were routed and much of Columbia was burned. General Edward Potter led a second force that destroyed cotton gins, railroads, and other property from Georgetown to Sumter to Camden.

POSTBELLUM LANDSCAPE

POPULATION, 1900

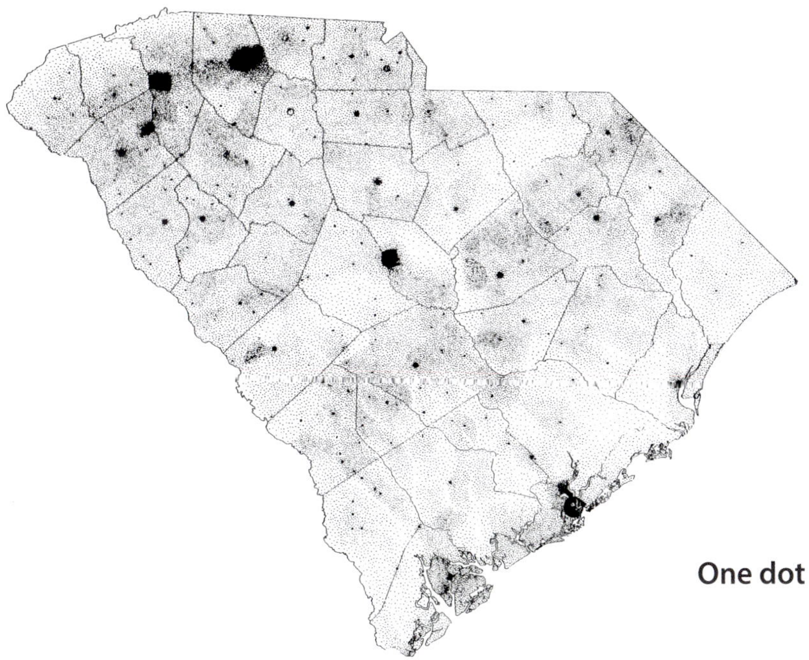

POPULATION, 1950

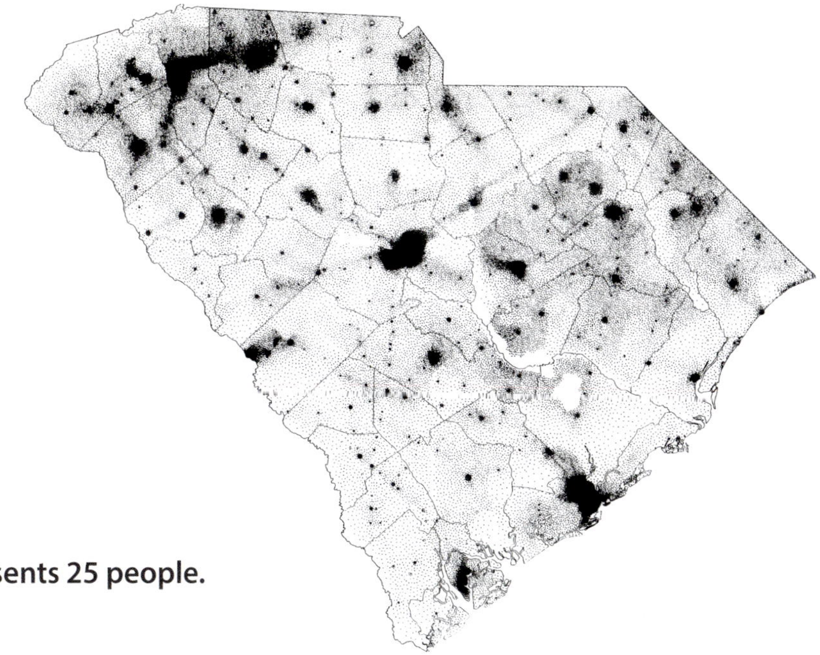

One dot represents 25 people.

The postbellum landscape after the Civil War saw many changes: increased cultivation of cotton, the rise of tenant farming, large-scale migration of Black people from the state, and a growing trend of rural-to-urban migration. At the beginning of the twentieth century the state's population stood at 1,340,000. This number would climb to 2,117,000 by 1950. These maps show the rapid growth of urban areas. The 1950 map shows "blank" spaces in the Inner Coastal Plain, which are reservoirs. The growth of towns created a demand for electricity. While the earliest hydroelectric plants were constructed in the 1890s, rivers were dammed to create large reservoirs like Lakes Greenwood, Murray, Marion, and Moultrie in the 1930s and early 1940s. While South Carolina's population tripled from 1870 to 1950, this growth lagged far behind the nation's growth and exceeded the national growth rate only twice during this period. South Carolina received little of the great wave of European immigrants between 1880 and 1920, and like other Southern states, South Carolina was not part of the traditional "melting pot."

BLACK POPULATION 1900–1940

Early in the twentieth century, many Black communities faced poverty and discrimination in South Carolina's segregated society. Black people left the state in large numbers between 1900 and 1940, seeking better lives and livelihoods in northern cities. More than half a million Black people migrated out of South Carolina during this period, known as the Great Migration. While the White population increased by nearly 70 percent, outmigration held Black population growth to only 1 percent between 1900 and 1930. This caused a shift from a Black population majority that existed between 1820 and 1920 to a White majority since 1920. Black outmigration was strongest in the rural lower Piedmont and southern Coastal Plain regions.

BLACK POPULATION, 1930

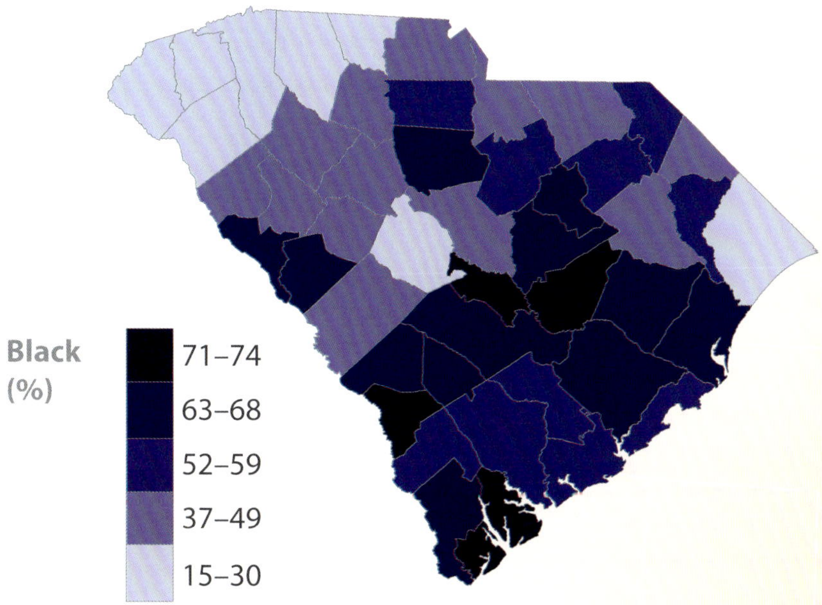

BLACK OUTMIGRATION, 1930

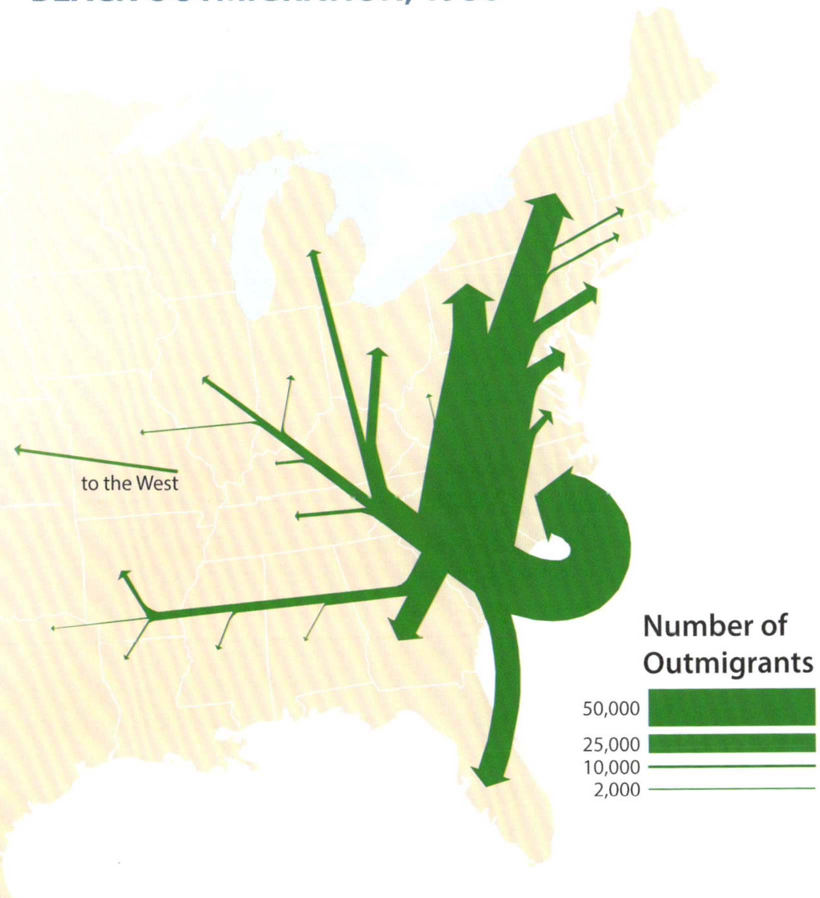

TENANCY AND TOBACCO

Between the Civil War and World War II, South Carolina was a rural agricultural state dominated by cotton, tobacco, farm tenancy, and a weak economy. While cotton was important throughout the period, it reached its maximum production in 1920. Tobacco became a significant cash crop around the turn of the century, but it was primarily a regional Pee Dee crop by the 1930s. Both cotton and tobacco crops demanded a great deal of labor. Tenancy replaced slavery as a labor system. Landowners supplied tenants with land, housing, and farming equipment in exchange for their labor. Tenants often paid high rents, became trapped in debt, and had little control over the crops they produced. Tenants operated nearly two-thirds of the state's farms in the 1930s and over one-half as late as World War II. Because of the state's agricultural labor system and low cotton prices, per capita income was only about half the national average in 1940.

TENANTS AS A PERCENT OF FARM OPERATORS, 1935

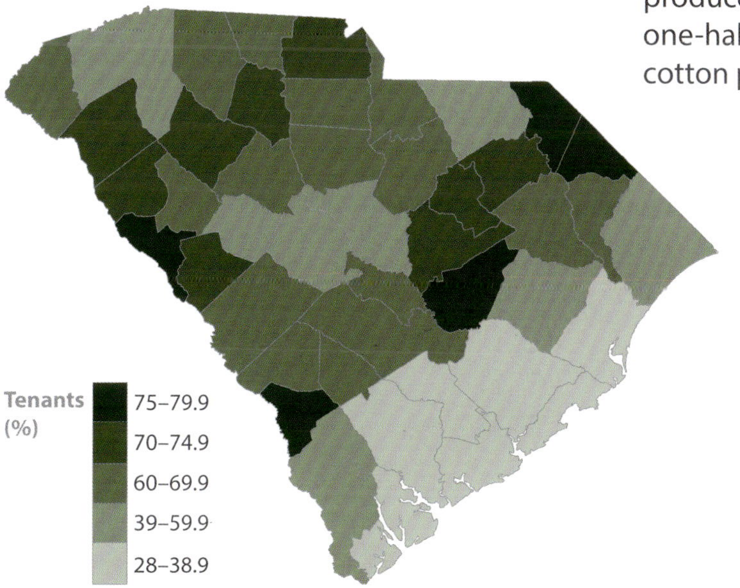

TOBACCO PRODUCTION, 1930

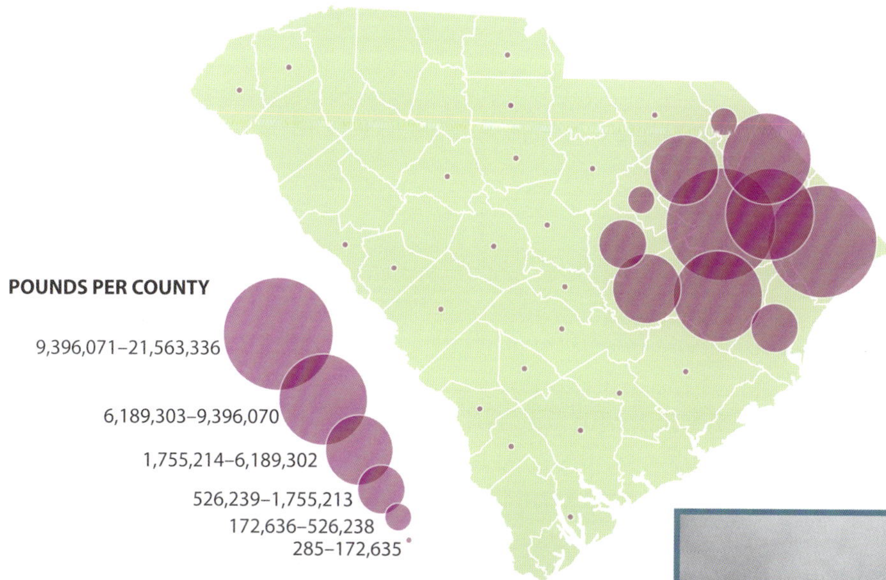

Wealthy landlords controlled many aspects of their tenant's daily lives and labor. While sharecroppers could try to move in search of better living and working conditions, it was not easy. Pictured here is a tenant farmer in 1941 moving his belongings out of the Camp Croft area near Pacolet in Spartanburg County.

Tobacco curing barns once dotted the Pee Dee region. This barn in Hartsville, ca. 1938, is typical of early structures. Tobacco leaves were sorted and then hung inside to cure. Here, tobacco is brought in from the field on a small skid. Unlike wheels, the ski-like runners kept the skid from becoming stuck in the mud.

TEXTILES AND RAILROADS

South Carolina's textile industry grew from 18 mills in the 1880s to nearly 150 mills by 1910. This growth was fueled by abundant water power for electricity generation, ample raw material (short-staple cotton), inexpensive labor, and the expansion of railroads. Most mills were in the upper Piedmont counties of Oconee, Anderson, Greenville and Spartanburg, but some mills were in the Midlands, including Graniteville in Aiken County. Mill village residents soon represented 10 percent of South Carolina's total population. By the 1920s, the railroad system expanded to connect South Carolina to Northeastern and Midwestern cities, shifting the focus away from Charleston. The expanded rail system also impacted the development of towns. Like beads on a string radiating from the state's major cities, numerous commercial towns developed along the new rail lines.

TEXTILE MILL LOCATIONS, 1908

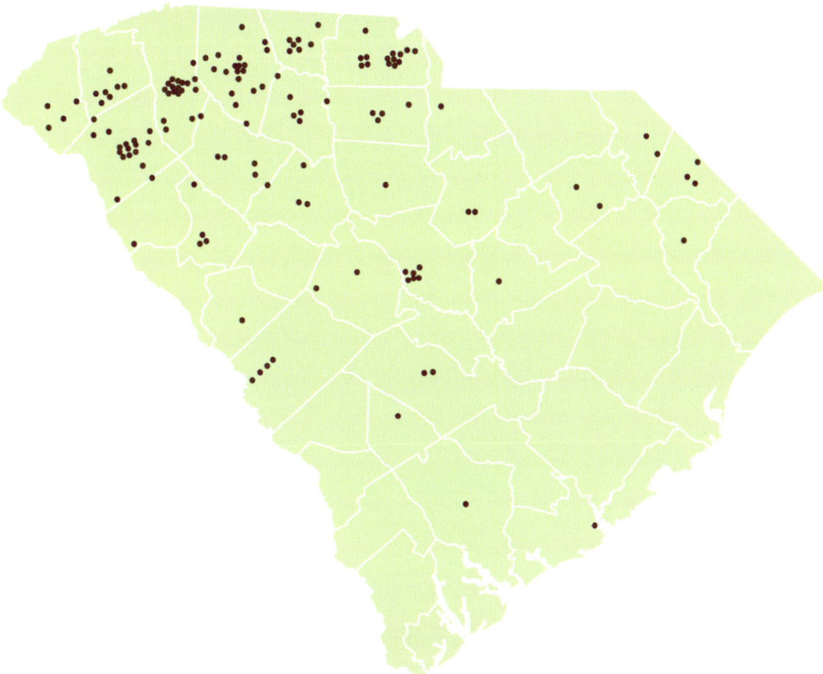

RAILROADS, 1925

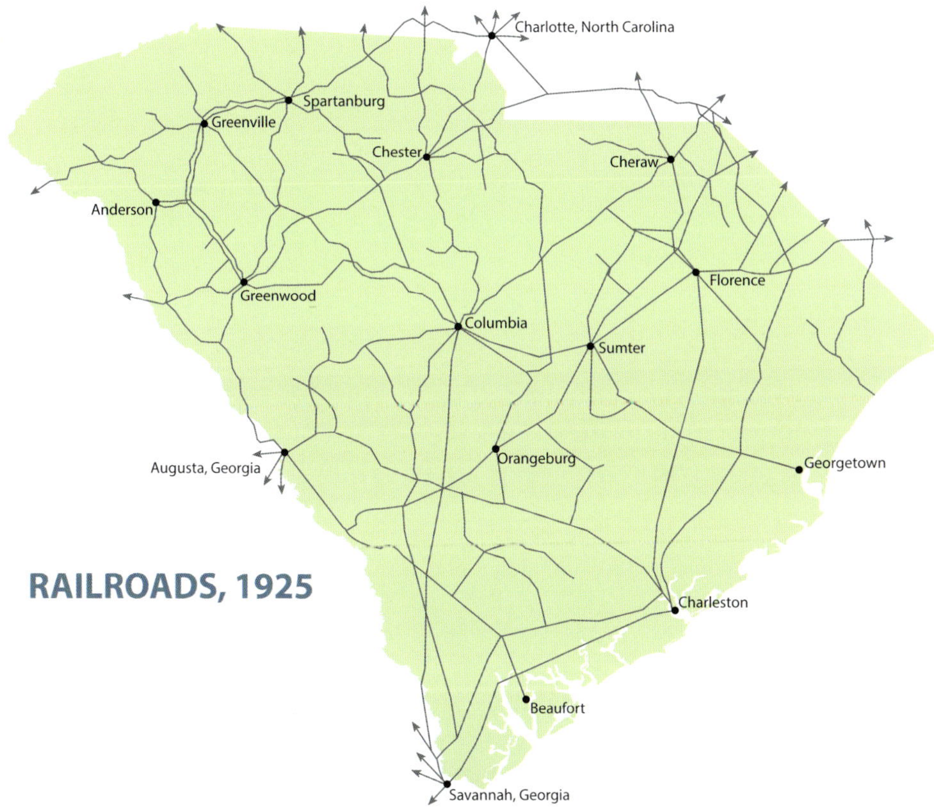

Graniteville was William Gregg's vision of a mill village—an assemblage of houses, schools, churches, and stores. The original mill was constructed of locally quarried granite and completed in 1849. A series of small houses designed in Early Gothic Revival Style dot the hillside. Children were educated at a school run and financed by the mill company. Changes in the global economy resulted in many textile mills closing across the state, which has hurt the economic stability of former mill villages.

CIVIL RIGHTS ERA

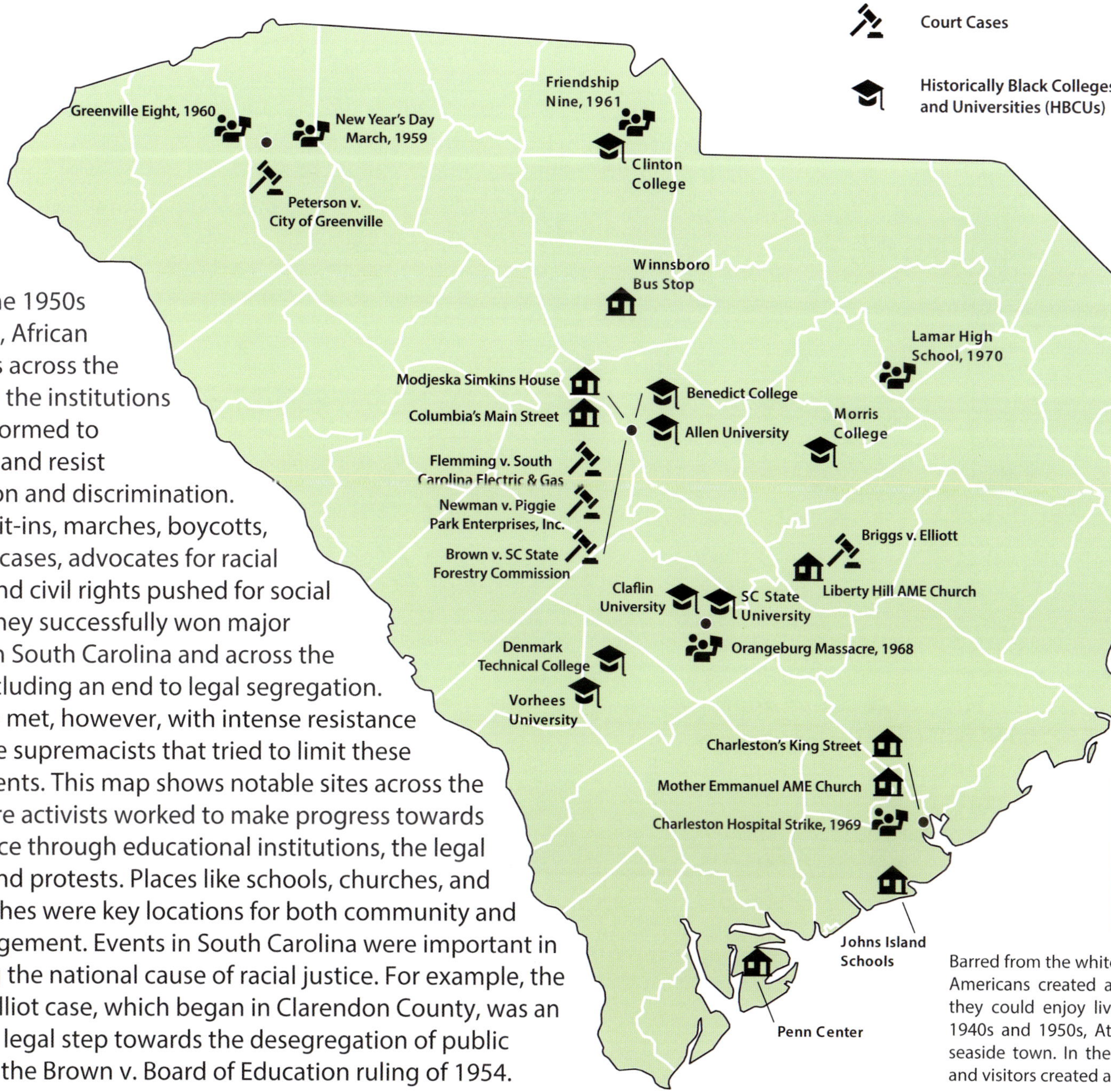

During the 1950s and 1960s, African Americans across the state used the institutions they had formed to challenge and resist segregation and discrimination. Through sit-ins, marches, boycotts, and court cases, advocates for racial equality and civil rights pushed for social change. They successfully won major changes in South Carolina and across the nation, including an end to legal segregation. They were met, however, with intense resistance from white supremacists that tried to limit these achievements. This map shows notable sites across the state where activists worked to make progress towards racial justice through educational institutions, the legal process, and protests. Places like schools, churches, and even beaches were key locations for both community and civic engagement. Events in South Carolina were important in advancing the national cause of racial justice. For example, the Briggs v. Elliot case, which began in Clarendon County, was an important legal step towards the desegregation of public schools in the Brown v. Board of Education ruling of 1954.

Barred from the white beaches in Myrtle Beach, African Americans created an enclave within the city where they could enjoy living and vacationing. During the 1940s and 1950s, Atlantic Beach became a booming seaside town. In the face of discrimination, residents and visitors created a vibrant community.

7 CONTEMPORARY LANDSCAPE

POPULATION, 2020

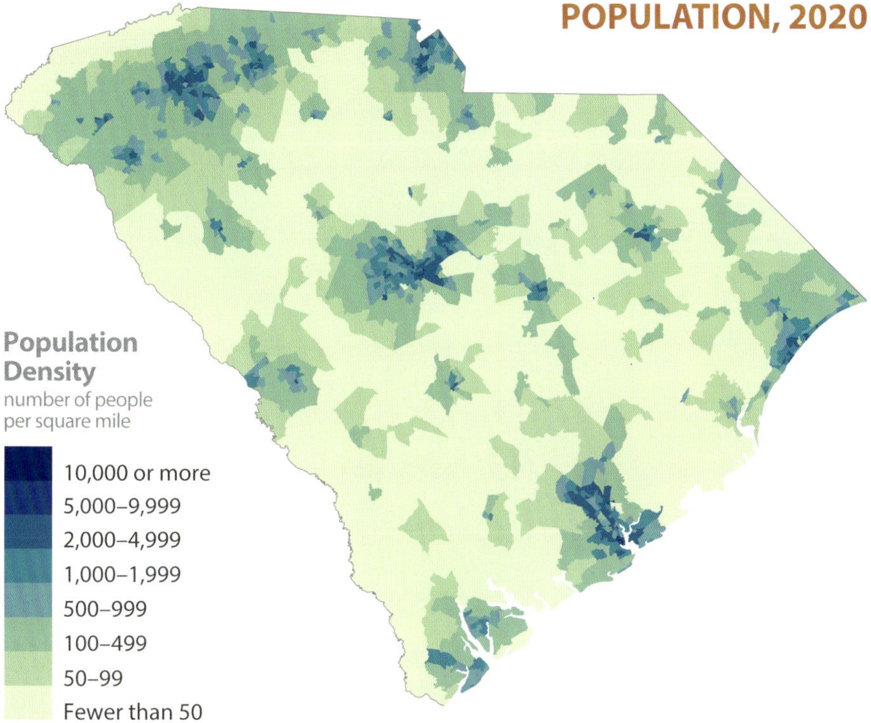

The interstate highway system allowed access to the state's larger cities, and the small compact cities of the 1950s gave way to sprawling suburbanized metropolitan areas. Tourism and a growing retiree population have caused some coastal counties, especially Horry and Beaufort, to join suburban counties such as Berkeley, Dorchester, Lexington, and York as high growth areas. South Carolina has also attracted new residents to urban centers like Greenville, Charleston, Columbia, and the outskirts of Charlotte (NC). However, rural counties and many small towns located on state highways have not shared in this growth and many have lost population.

South Carolina's population nearly doubled between 1970 and 2020, reaching over 5 million people. The decade of the 1970s, however, stands out as the most important decade of the twentieth century with respect to landscape and lifestyle change in South Carolina. It was during the 1970s when South Carolina began to experience the "Sunbelt" or "New South" population and economic growth: segregation ended; urban dwellers first outnumbered rural residents; the interstate highway system was being completed; new industries were aggressively recruited. Since then, South Carolina has grown by about half a million people every ten years.

POPULATION CHANGE, 1970–2020

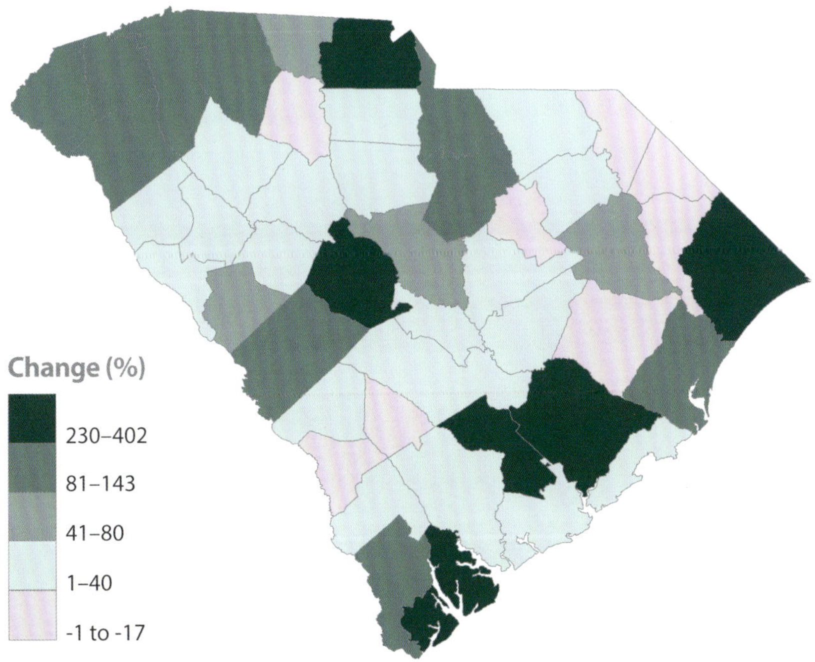

CITIES AND METROPOLITAN STATISTICAL AREAS

As of 2020, there were 204 census designated places in South Carolina. These are unincorporated but locally recognized communities. Over 90 percent of census designated places have populations of 10,000 or fewer. Larger populations live in incorporated towns and cities across the state. The largest city in the state is Charleston, with just over 150,000 residents. Columbia is the second largest city. South Carolina cities are relatively small. Most US metropolitan areas have suburbs with more people than the largest South Carolina cities.

METROPOLITAN STATISTICAL AREAS

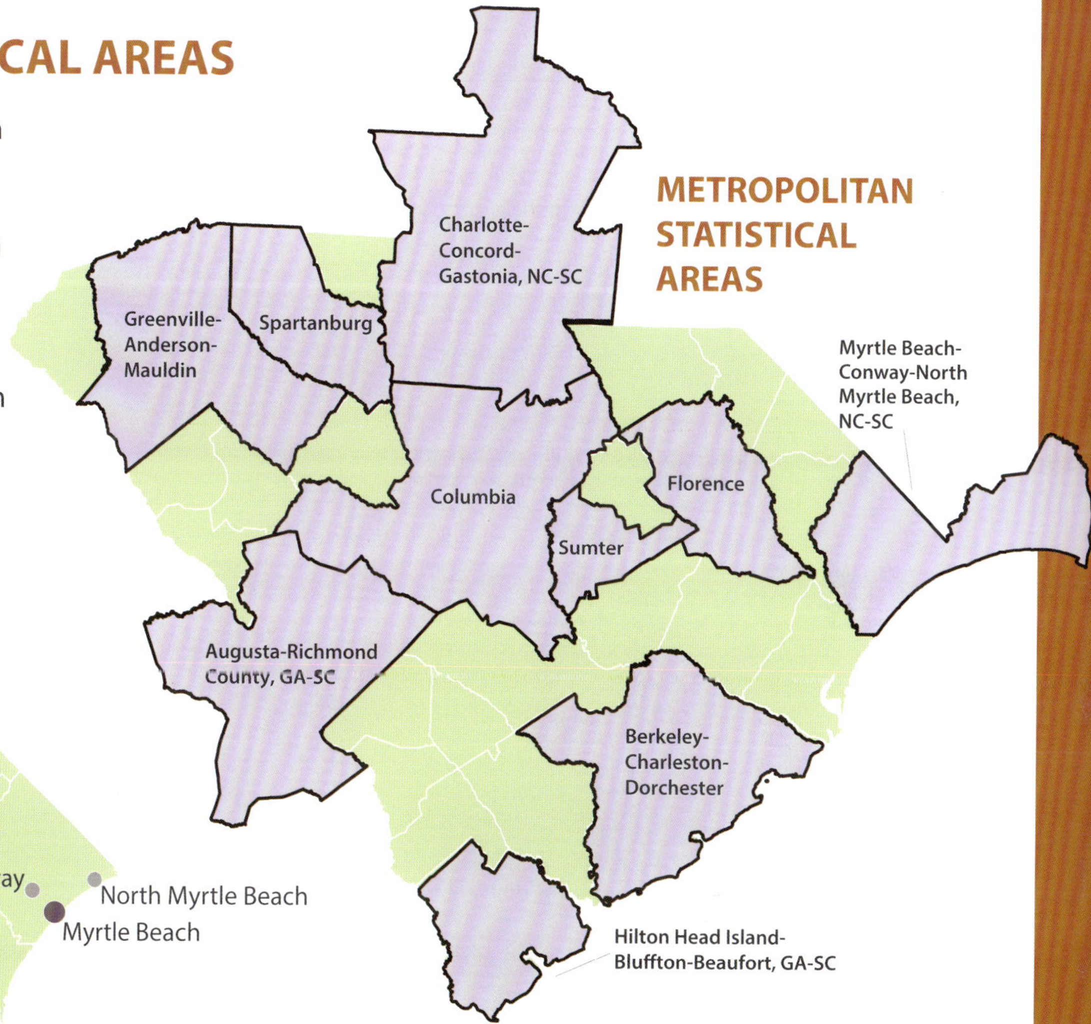

CITIES

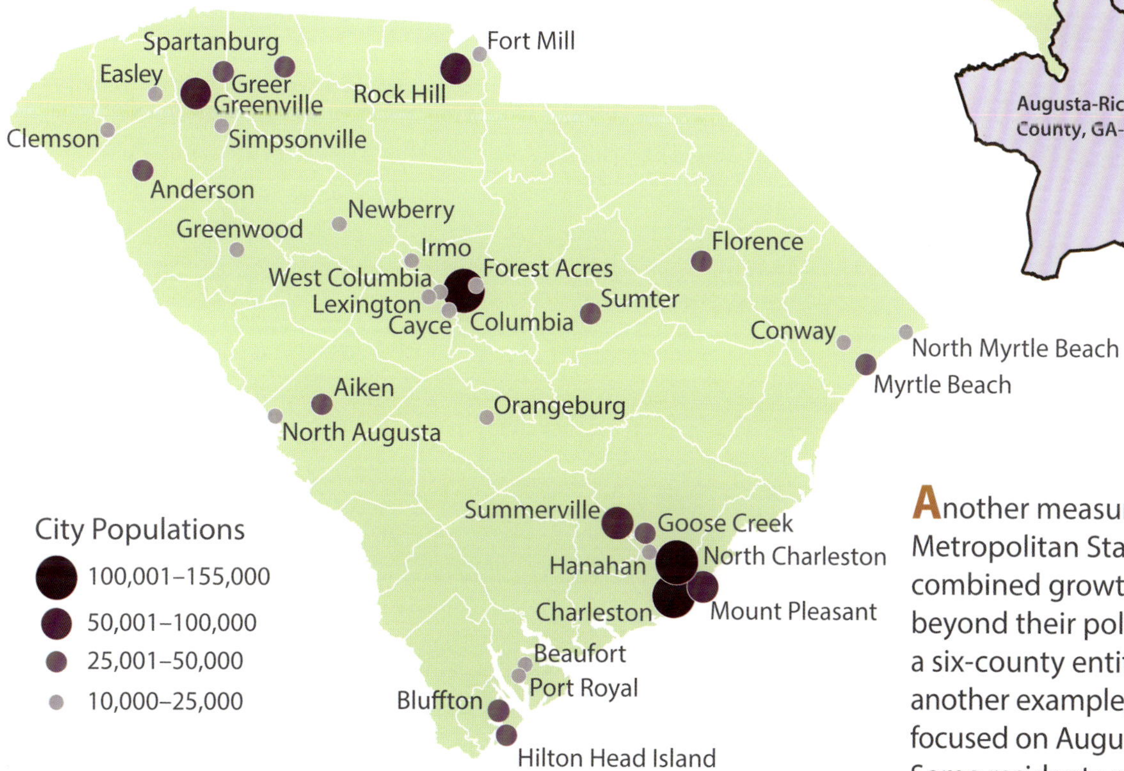

Another measure for population and economic integration is the Metropolitan Statistical Area (MSA). An MSA is a way to measure combined growth of areas, recognizing the influence of cities far beyond their political borders. For example, Columbia is shown as a six-county entity that accounts for more than 830,000 people. In another example, the Augusta-Richmond County MSA, while focused on Augusta, Georgia, includes Aiken and Edgefield counties. Some residents of these two counties commute to work and shop in the Georgia city although the river and state boundary intervene.

POPULATION BORN AND RESIDING IN SOUTH CAROLINA

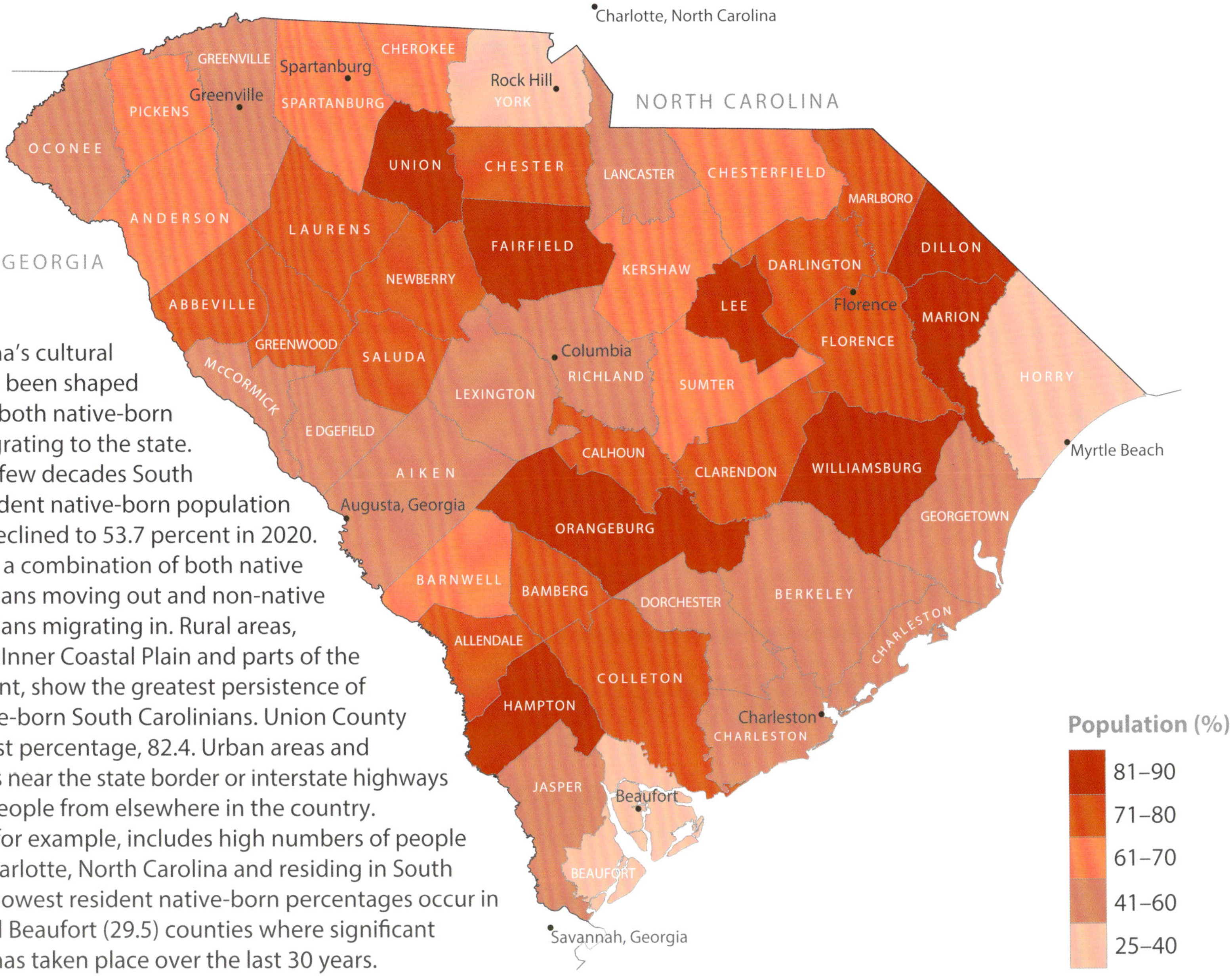

South Carolina's cultural landscape has been shaped by its people, both native-born and those migrating to the state. Over the past few decades South Carolina's resident native-born population has steadily declined to 53.7 percent in 2020. This decline is a combination of both native South Carolinians moving out and non-native South Carolinians migrating in. Rural areas, especially the Inner Coastal Plain and parts of the lower Piedmont, show the greatest persistence of resident native-born South Carolinians. Union County has the highest percentage, 82.4. Urban areas and some counties near the state border or interstate highways have drawn people from elsewhere in the country. York County, for example, includes high numbers of people working in Charlotte, North Carolina and residing in South Carolina. The lowest resident native-born percentages occur in Horry (35) and Beaufort (29.5) counties where significant in-migration has taken place over the last 30 years.

RACE AND ETHNICITY

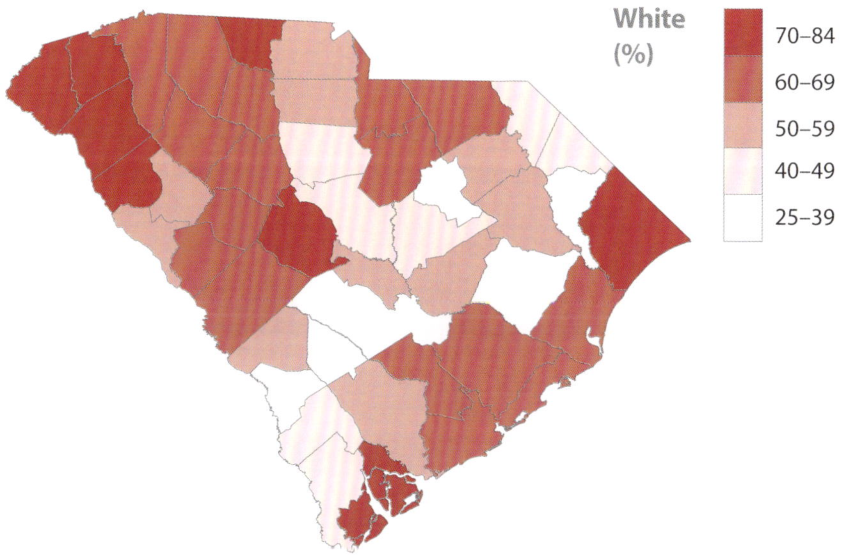

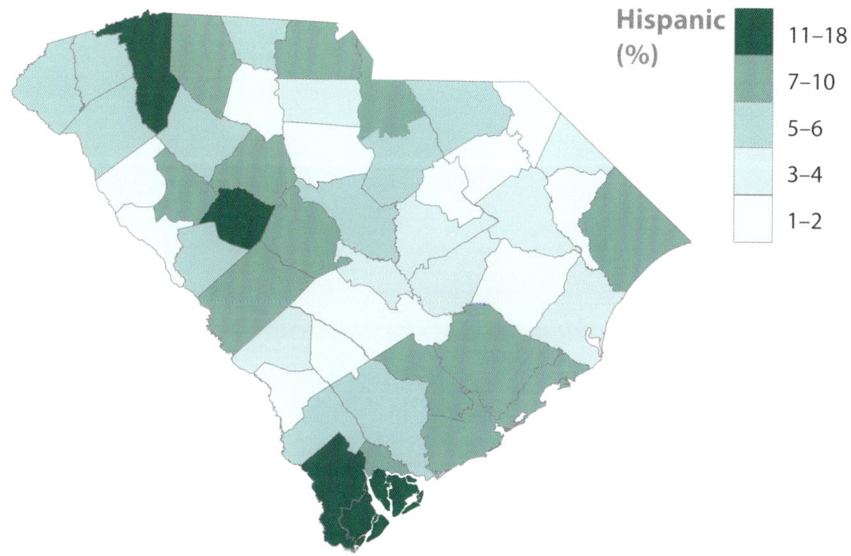

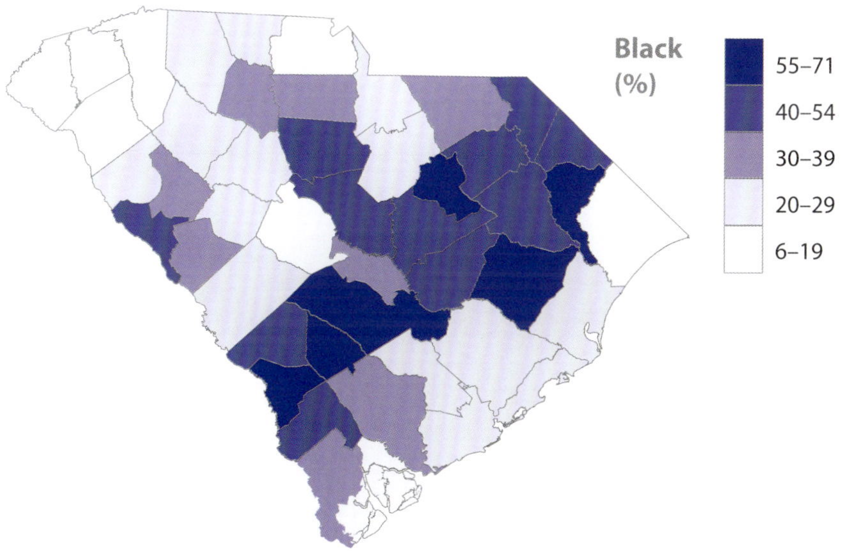

South Carolina is approximately 63 percent White and 25 percent Black, giving the state one of the highest minority population percentages in the country. Hispanic population growth has been considerable in recent decades. At the county level, the Upstate is predominately White and the Inner Coastal Plain is generally Black. The Midlands and coastal regions are mixed. These patterns vary as geographic scale changes. For example, Black populations in the Upstate are concentrated around cities like Greenville but are more dispersed in the rural counties of the Coastal Plain. Native Americans and Asians are small in number, with the former concentrated near Dillon, Dorchester, and York counties and the latter in urban areas. South Carolina has one federally recognized tribe, the Catawba Indian Nation, with over 3,300 enrolled members located along the banks of the Catawba River near Rock Hill.

EDUCATION

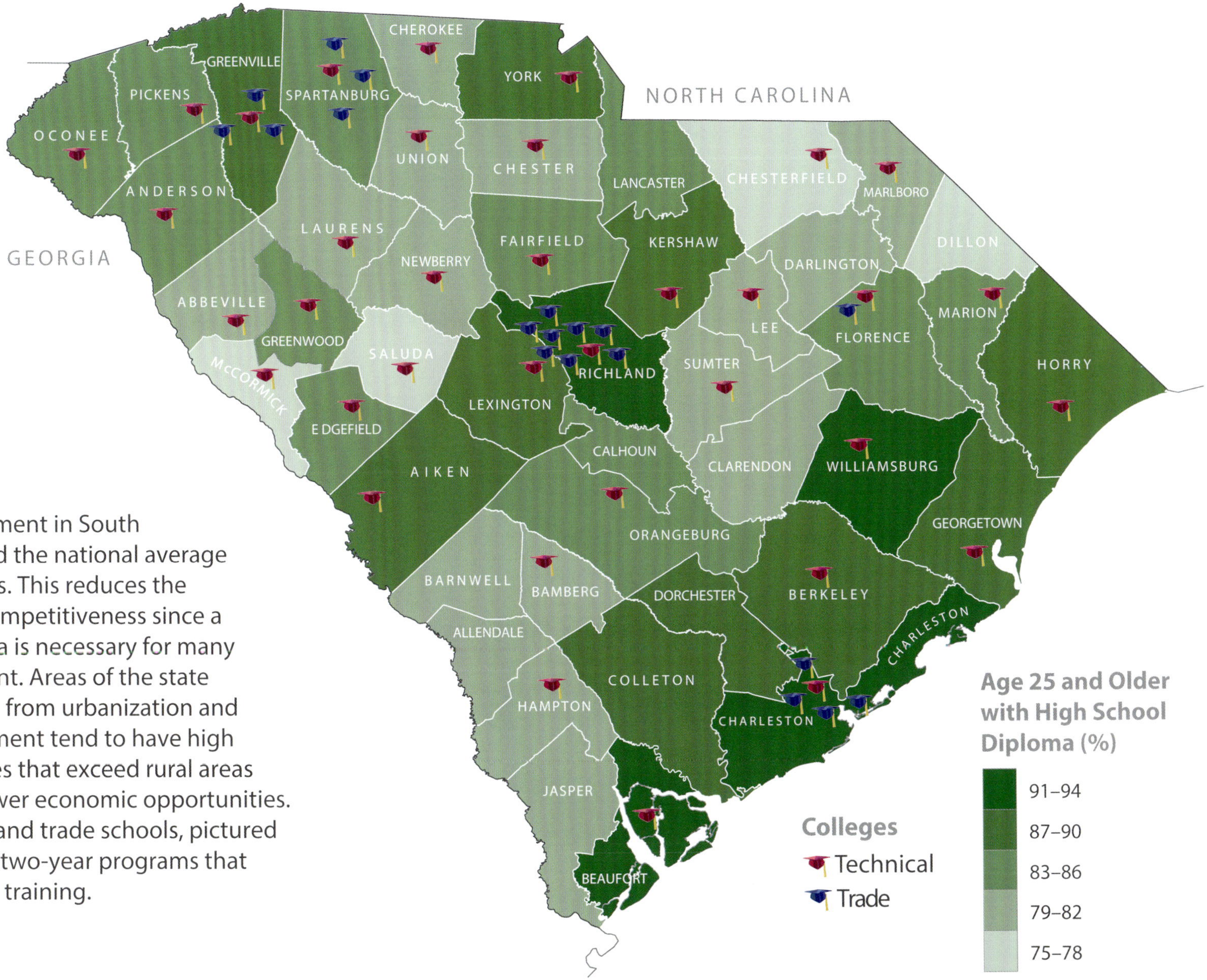

Educational attainment in South Carolina lags behind the national average in several categories. This reduces the state's economic competitiveness since a high school diploma is necessary for many types of employment. Areas of the state that have benefited from urbanization and economic development tend to have high school diploma rates that exceed rural areas of the state with fewer economic opportunities. Technical Colleges and trade schools, pictured here, typically offer two-year programs that focus on vocational training.

HIGHER EDUCATION

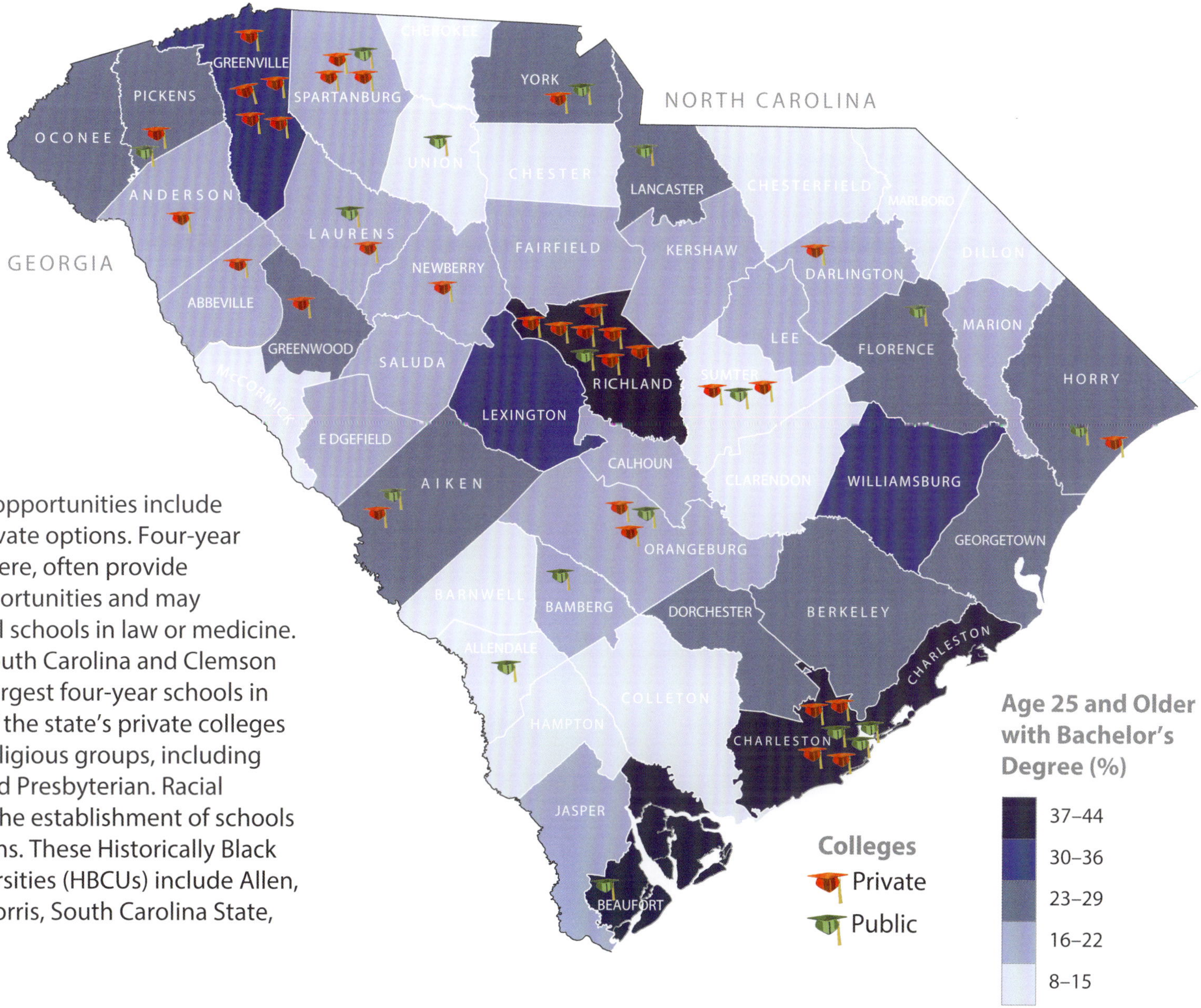

Higher education opportunities include both public and private options. Four-year colleges, pictured here, often provide graduate study opportunities and may include professional schools in law or medicine. The University of South Carolina and Clemson University are the largest four-year schools in the state. Several of the state's private colleges were founded by religious groups, including Erskine, Furman, and Presbyterian. Racial segregation led to the establishment of schools for African Americans. These Historically Black Colleges and Universities (HBCUs) include Allen, Benedict, Claflin, Morris, South Carolina State, and Voorhees.

MILITARY LANDSCAPE

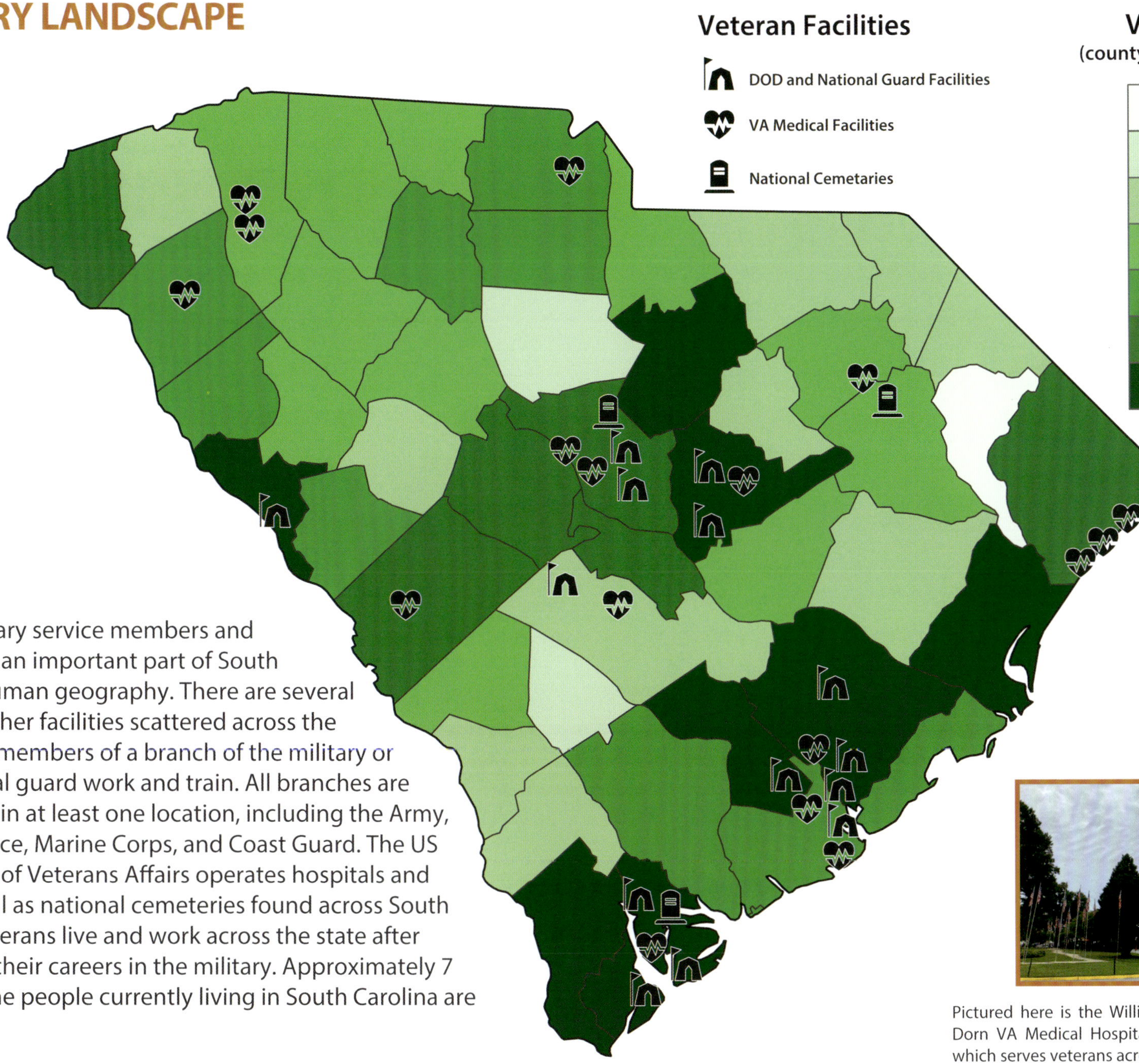

Active military service members and veterans are an important part of South Carolina's human geography. There are several bases and other facilities scattered across the state where members of a branch of the military or state national guard work and train. All branches are represented in at least one location, including the Army, Navy, Air Force, Marine Corps, and Coast Guard. The US Department of Veterans Affairs operates hospitals and clinics as well as national cemeteries found across South Carolina. Veterans live and work across the state after completing their careers in the military. Approximately 7 percent of the people currently living in South Carolina are veterans.

Pictured here is the William Jennings Bryan Dorn VA Medical Hospital in Columbia, SC, which serves veterans across the state.

AGRICULTURE

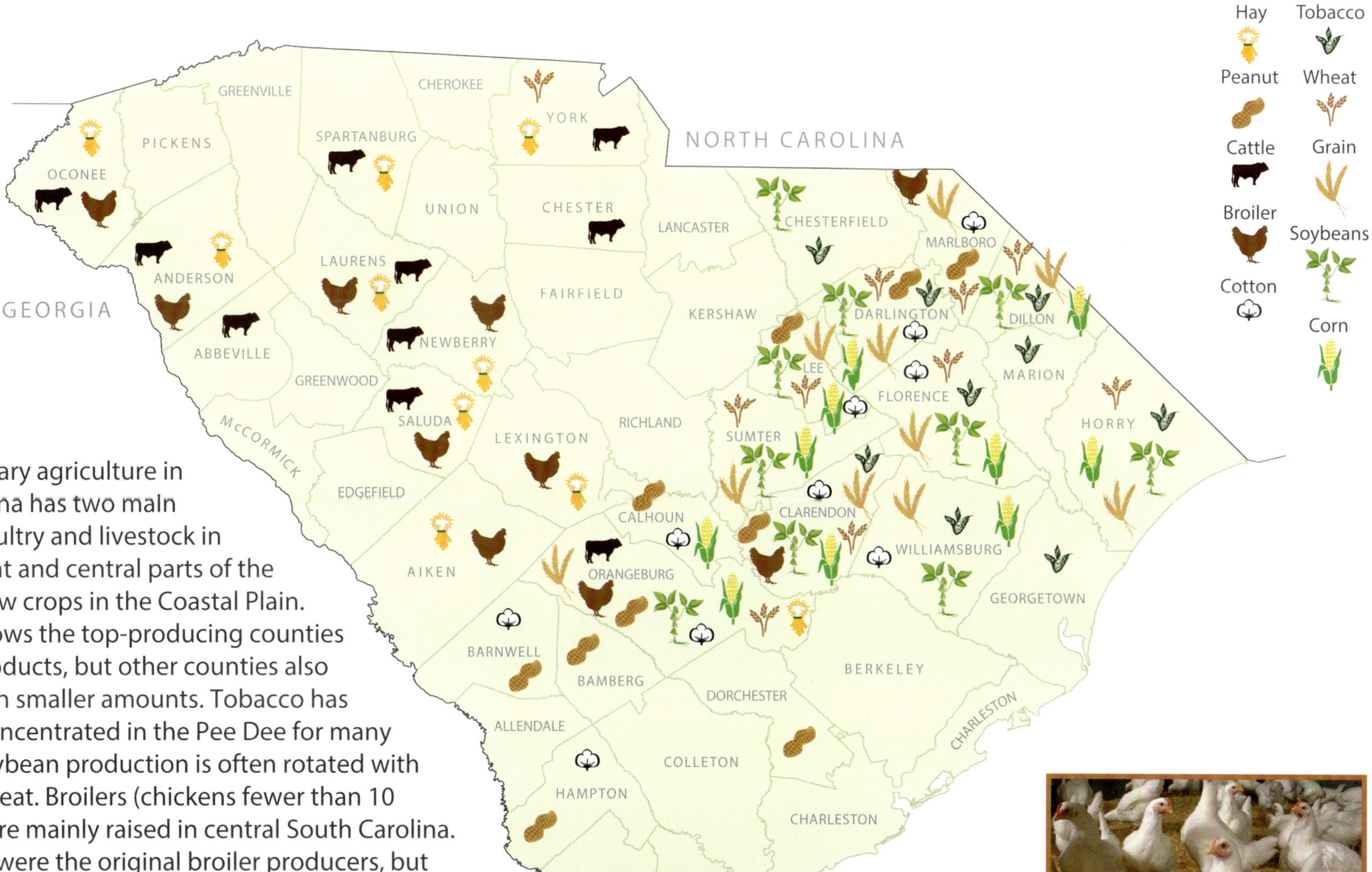

Contemporary agriculture in South Carolina has two main patterns: poultry and livestock in the Piedmont and central parts of the state, and row crops in the Coastal Plain. The map shows the top-producing counties for these products, but other counties also grow them in smaller amounts. Tobacco has remained concentrated in the Pee Dee for many decades. Soybean production is often rotated with corn and wheat. Broilers (chickens fewer than 10 weeks old) are mainly raised in central South Carolina. Small farms were the original broiler producers, but many operations have expanded; the long, one-story broiler house is now a common landscape feature. Cotton production increased during the 1990s after a decades-long decline. Although no longer a Piedmont crop, cotton remains in the Coastal Plain. Piedmont land that formerly grew cotton is now used for forage, small-scale cattle rearing, and pine forests.

Broiler houses can contain thousands of birds like these pictured here. Large companies own the flocks, feed mills, and processing plants, and the farmer, under contract, grows the chicks. Broilers have become a leading farm commodity in South Carolina.

INDUSTRY

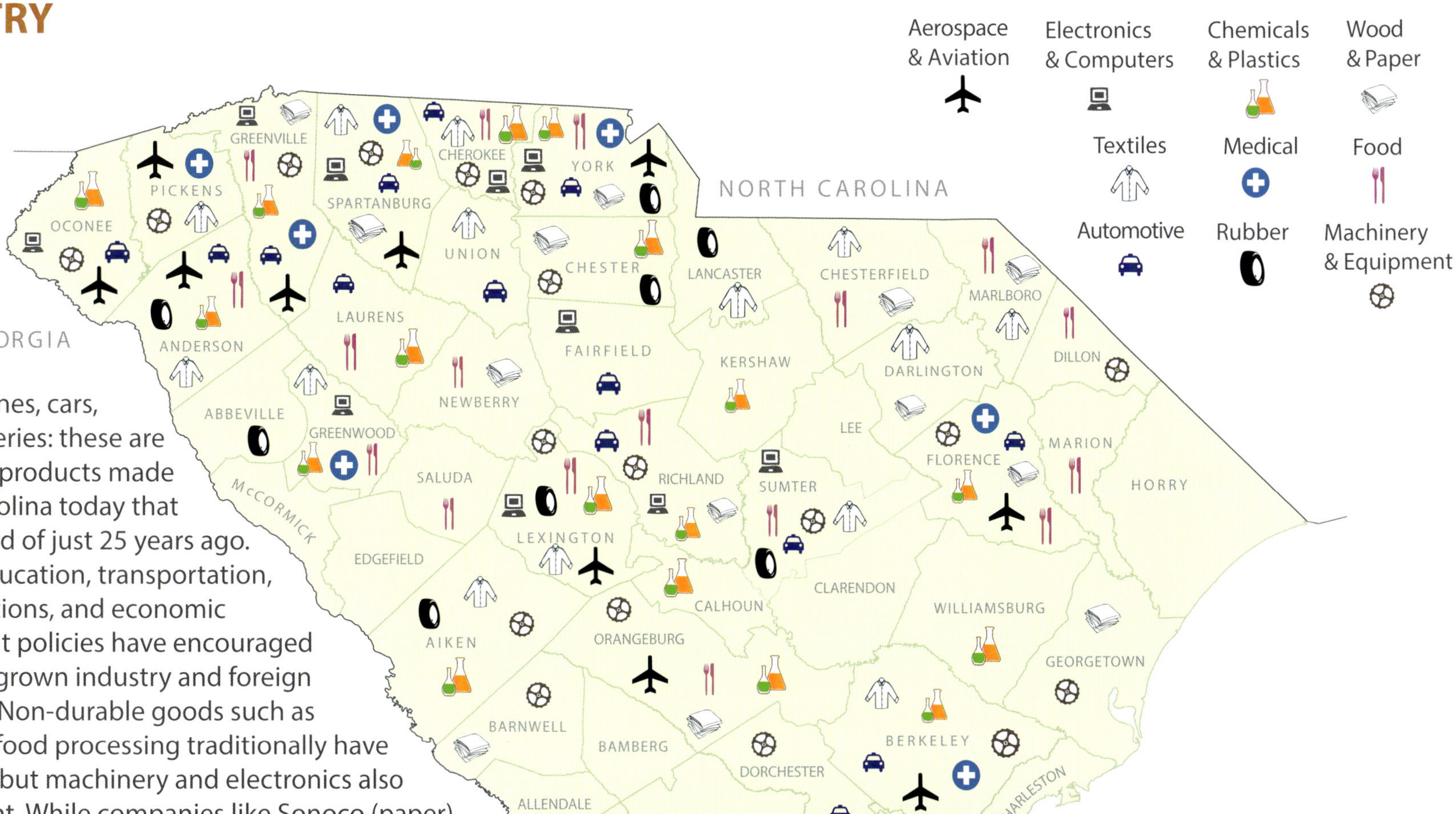

Tires, airplanes, cars, electric batteries: these are some of the products made in South Carolina today that were unheard of just 25 years ago. Technical education, transportation, communications, and economic development policies have encouraged both home-grown industry and foreign investment. Non-durable goods such as textiles and food processing traditionally have led the way, but machinery and electronics also are important. While companies like Sonoco (paper) and Milliken (chemical) are headquartered in the state, other highly visible manufacturers include BMW and Volvo (cars), Boeing (airplanes), and Michelin (tires). The map shows industrial facilities employing more than 500 workers. Advanced manufacturing is concentrated in the Upstate and the Lowcountry. Companies choose to locate facilities near transportation networks, like rail lines and interstate highways, that help them move their products. For example, a string of facilities follows Interstate 85 and creates a manufacturing corridor that links Atlanta, Anderson, Greenville, Spartanburg, Gaffney, and Charlotte.

Steel rebar—reinforcing bar—is one of many industrial items manufactured in South Carolina. At CMC Steel in Cayce, rebar is made for residential and commercial construction and highways. The company has mills in eight other states and much of their production is from recycled scrap metal.

TRANSPORTATION

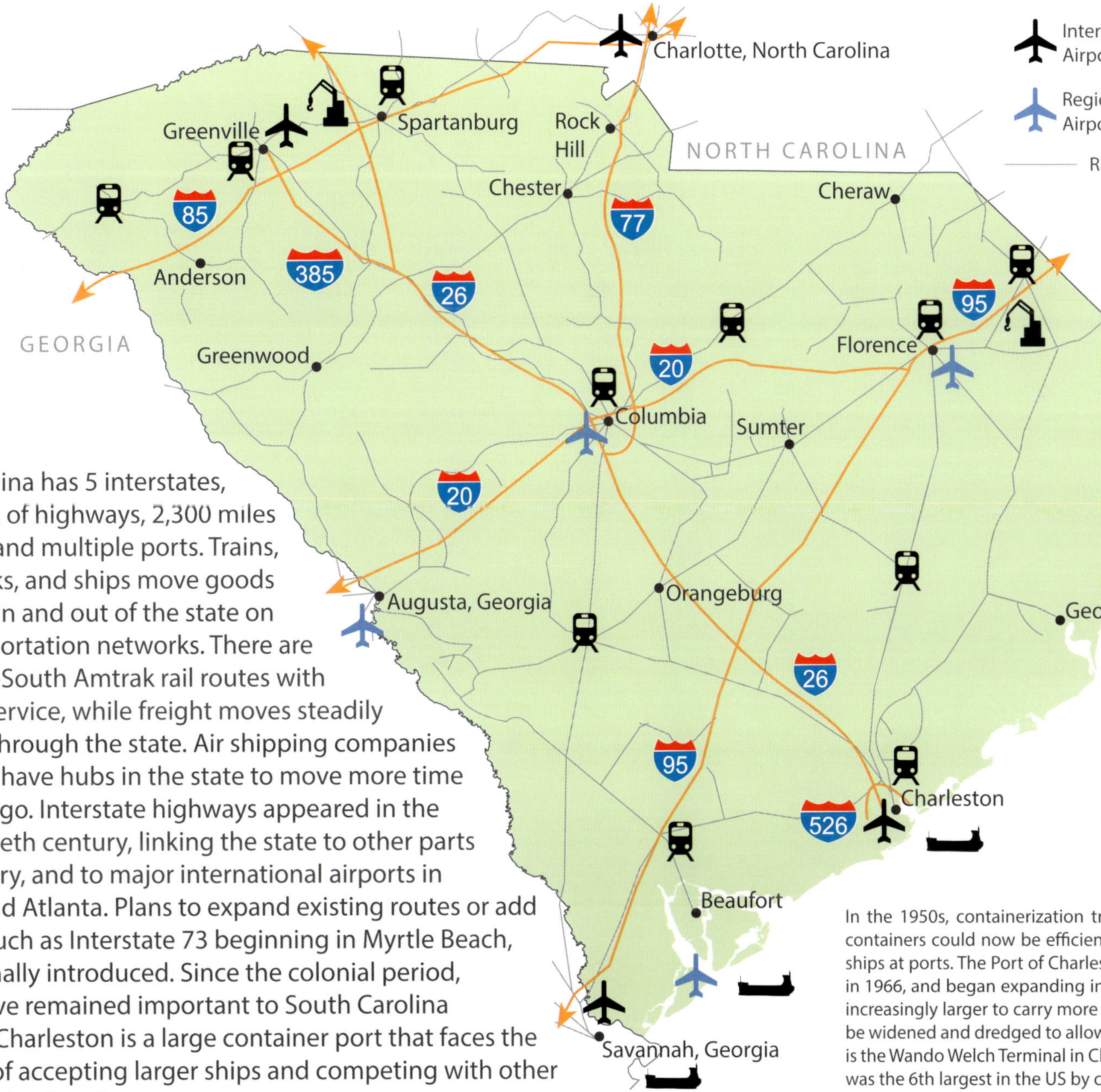

South Carolina has 5 interstates, 41,000 miles of highways, 2,300 miles of rail lines, and multiple ports. Trains, planes, trucks, and ships move goods and people in and out of the state on these transportation networks. There are three North-South Amtrak rail routes with passenger service, while freight moves steadily within and through the state. Air shipping companies such as UPS have hubs in the state to move more time sensitive cargo. Interstate highways appeared in the latter twentieth century, linking the state to other parts of the country, and to major international airports in Charlotte and Atlanta. Plans to expand existing routes or add new ones, such as Interstate 73 beginning in Myrtle Beach, are occasionally introduced. Since the colonial period, seaports have remained important to South Carolina commerce. Charleston is a large container port that faces the challenges of accepting larger ships and competing with other ports along the East Coast.

In the 1950s, containerization transformed global shipping. Entire containers could now be efficiently transferred between trucks and ships at ports. The Port of Charleston received its first container ship in 1966, and began expanding in 1970. Container ships have grown increasingly larger to carry more cargo. Ports and canals continue to be widened and dredged to allow larger ships to enter. Pictured here is the Wando Welch Terminal in Charleston. In 2020, Charleston's port was the 6th largest in the US by cargo value, moving over $72 billion in imports and exports.

ENERGY LANDSCAPE

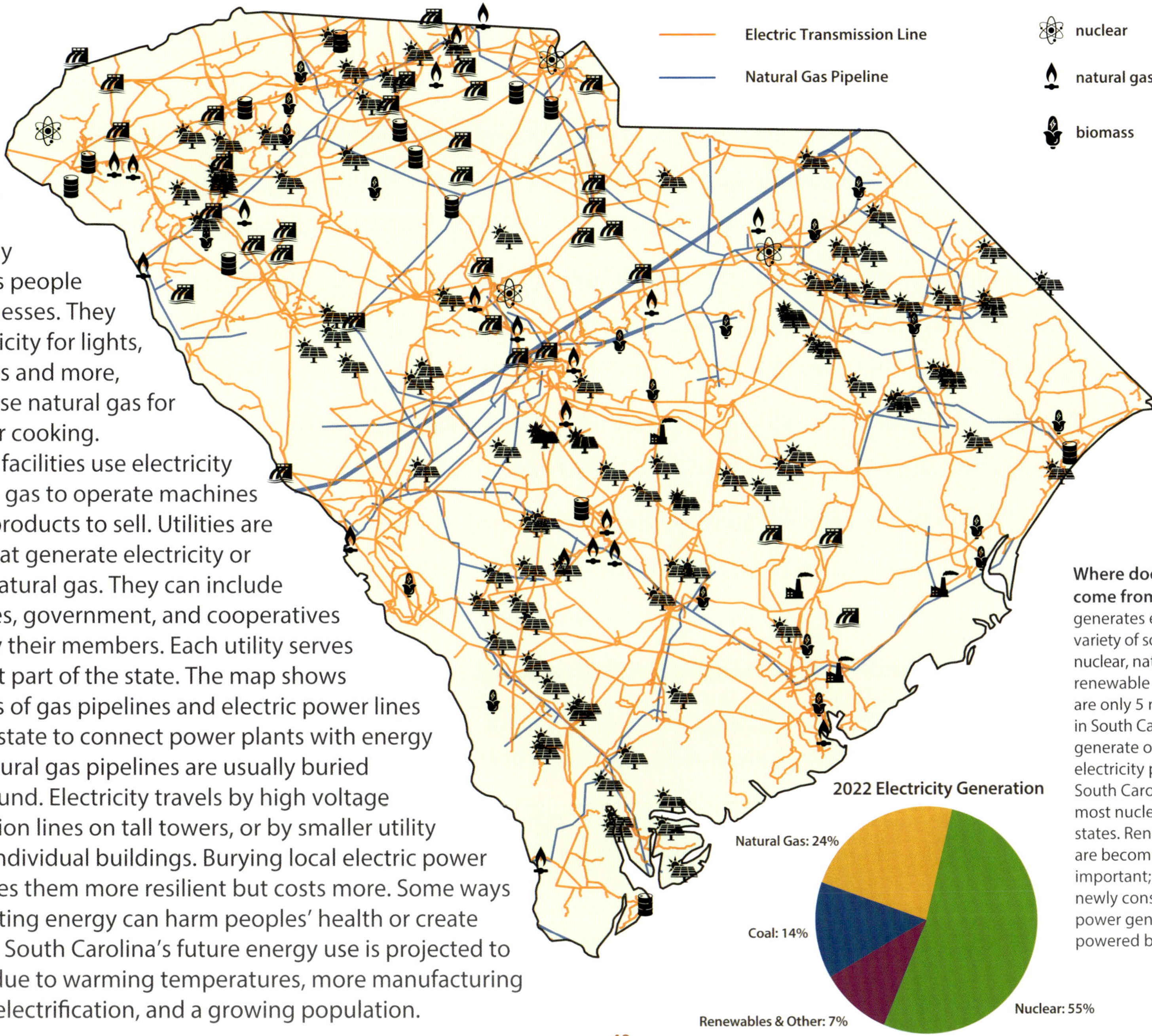

South Carolina's energy geography powers its people and businesses. They use electricity for lights, appliances and more, and can use natural gas for heating or cooking. Industrial facilities use electricity or natural gas to operate machines or make products to sell. Utilities are groups that generate electricity or transfer natural gas. They can include companies, government, and cooperatives owned by their members. Each utility serves a different part of the state. The map shows how webs of gas pipelines and electric power lines cross the state to connect power plants with energy users. Natural gas pipelines are usually buried underground. Electricity travels by high voltage transmission lines on tall towers, or by smaller utility poles to individual buildings. Burying local electric power lines makes them more resilient but costs more. Some ways of generating energy can harm peoples' health or create pollution. South Carolina's future energy use is projected to increase due to warming temperatures, more manufacturing facilities, electrification, and a growing population.

2022 Electricity Generation

Where does our electricity come from? South Carolina generates electricity from a variety of sources, including nuclear, natural gas, coal, and renewable energy. While there are only 5 nuclear power stations in South Carolina, they collectively generate over half of the electricity produced in the state. South Carolina produces the 3rd most nuclear energy of all US states. Renewable energy sources are becoming increasingly important; all of South Carolina's newly constructed utility-scale power generation in 2022 was powered by the sun.

STATE AND NATIONAL PARKS

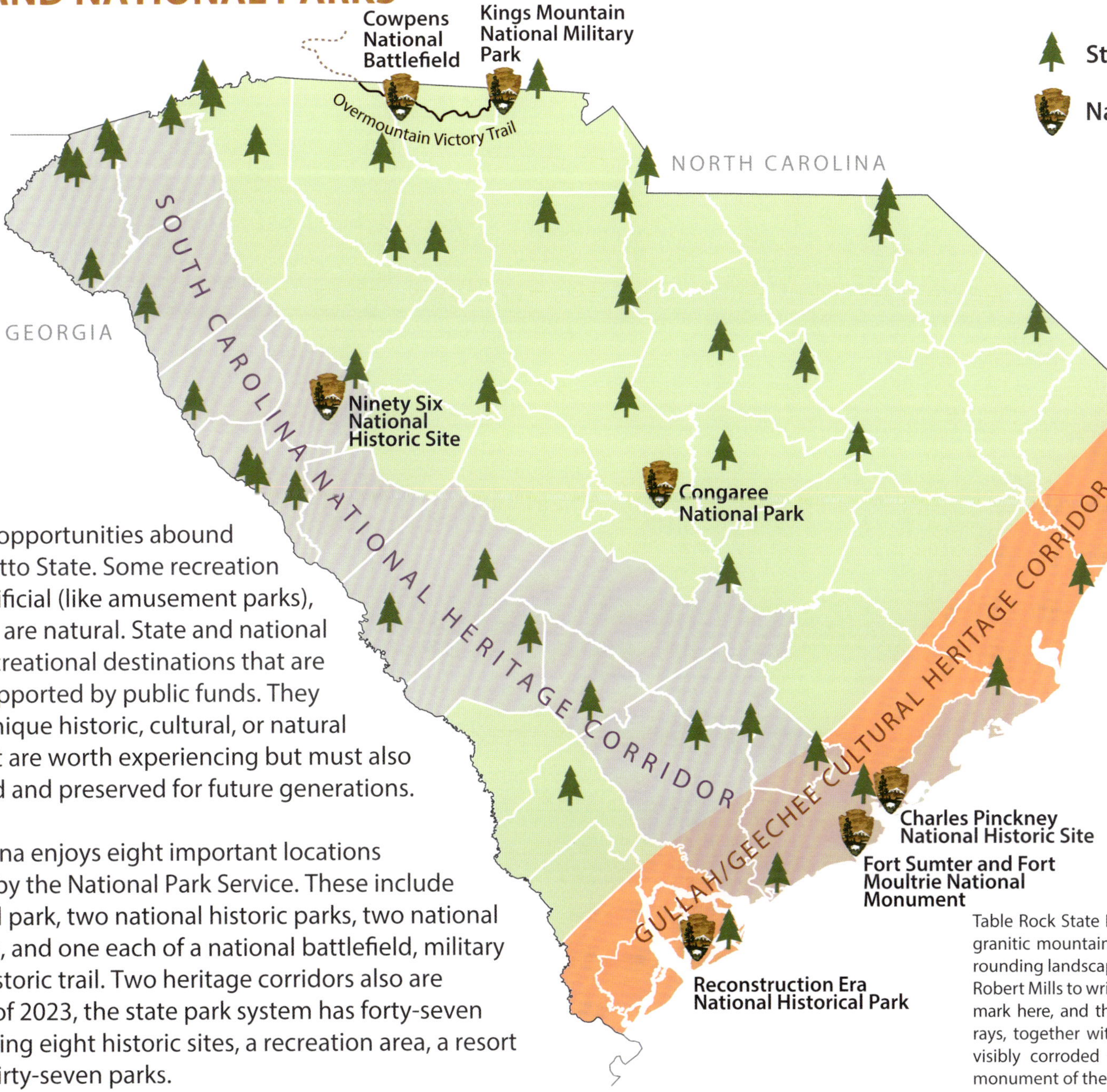

Recreation opportunities abound in the Palmetto State. Some recreation areas are artificial (like amusement parks), while others are natural. State and national parks are recreational destinations that are generally supported by public funds. They showcase unique historic, cultural, or natural features that are worth experiencing but must also be protected and preserved for future generations.

South Carolina enjoys eight important locations designated by the National Park Service. These include one national park, two national historic parks, two national historic sites, and one each of a national battlefield, military park, and historic trail. Two heritage corridors also are present. As of 2023, the state park system has forty-seven units, including eight historic sites, a recreation area, a resort park, and thirty-seven parks.

Table Rock State Park contains a monadnock, a granitic mountain feature rising above the surrounding landscape. The spectacular site moved Robert Mills to write that "Time alone has made a mark here, and the continual force of the sun's rays, together with the descending rains, have visibly corroded this apparently imperishable monument of the Deity."

TOURISM

South Carolina has many features that are attractive to both business and leisure travelers. Visitors spend money on goods and services such as restaurants, hotels, and transportation, which provides valuable income for the state. This tourism spending generated over $1.5 billion in tax revenue in 2019. Popular activities for visitors include going to the beach, visiting relatives, shopping, and dining out. Most visitors come from southern states such as North Carolina, Georgia, Virginia, and Florida. The vast majority of tourist expenditures (74 percent of the state total) occur in just five counties—Horry, Charleston, Beaufort, Greenville, and Richland. South Carolina's tourism industry was greatly impacted by the COVID-19 pandemic, shrinking by an estimated 31 percent in 2020.

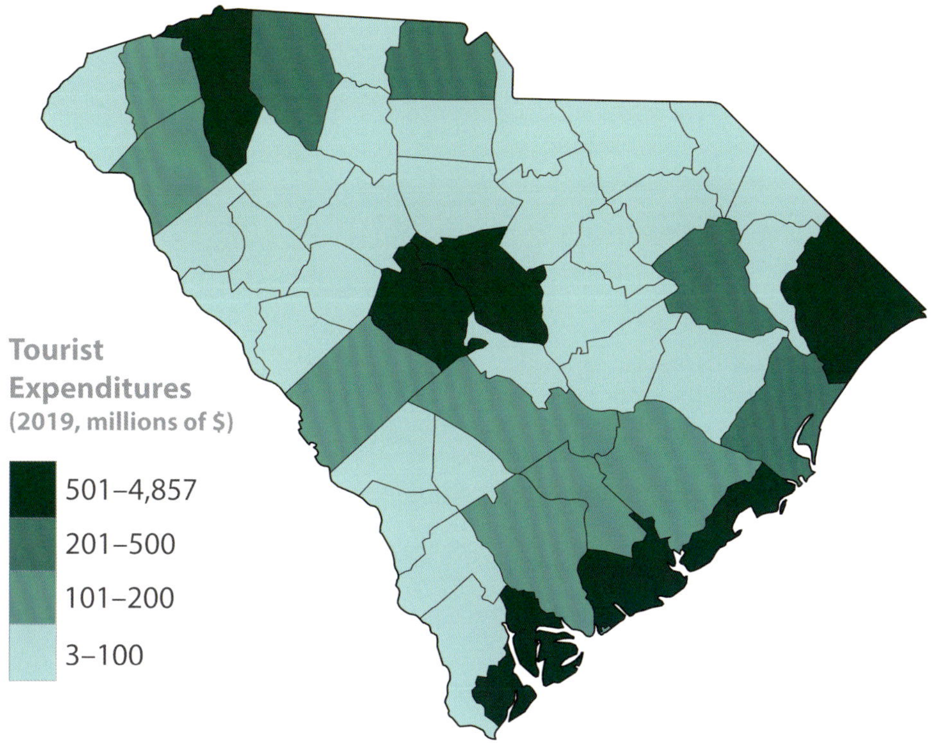

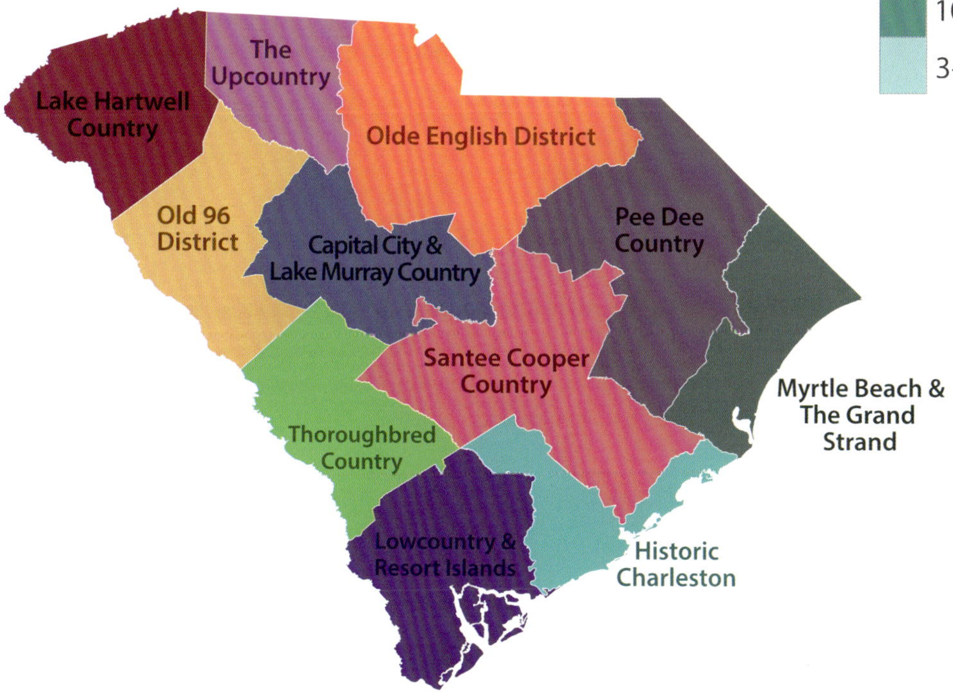

The state is divided into ten tourism regions which offer unique experiences for visitors. A hiking enthusiast? Try the Upcountry. Revolutionary War buff? The Old 96 or Olde English districts. Fishermen might enjoy Santee Cooper Country while NASCAR fans can take in a race in Pee Dee Country. Historic Charleston focuses on the charms of the old city and family fun and golf are major activities in Myrtle Beach and the Grand Strand. Various festivals are held in each region throughout every season and provide opportunities for year-round fun.

RELIGION

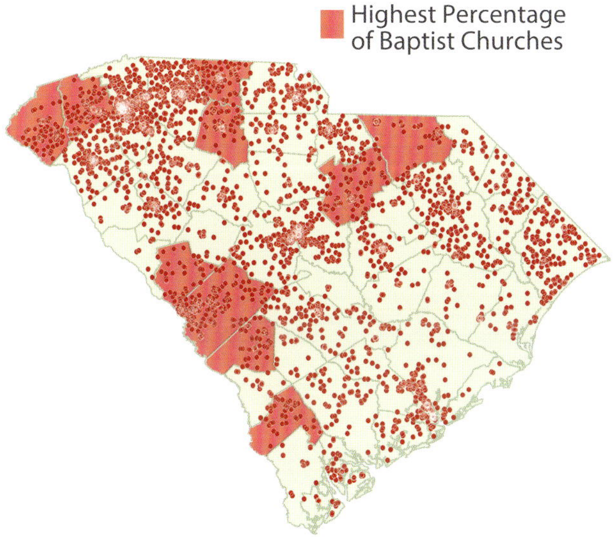

Religious life in South Carolina has been overwhelmingly Christian for the past 300 years. Four of the leading religious groups in the state are Baptist, Methodist, Presbyterian, and Lutheran.

Baptists, South Carolina's largest religious group, worship in more than 3,500 churches, nearly 40 percent of the total.

Methodist congregations, the second most numerous group, are located throughout the state and have a slightly higher concentration within the Coastal Plain.

Scotch-Irish migration in the mid-1700s resulted in more Presbyterian churches in the Catawba River valley and portions of the Upstate. German migration was responsible for a strong Lutheran presence that still exists in Lexington, Newberry, and Saluda counties.

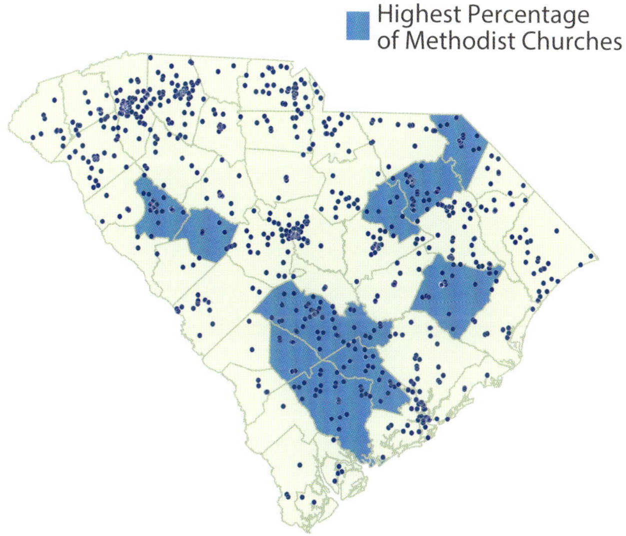

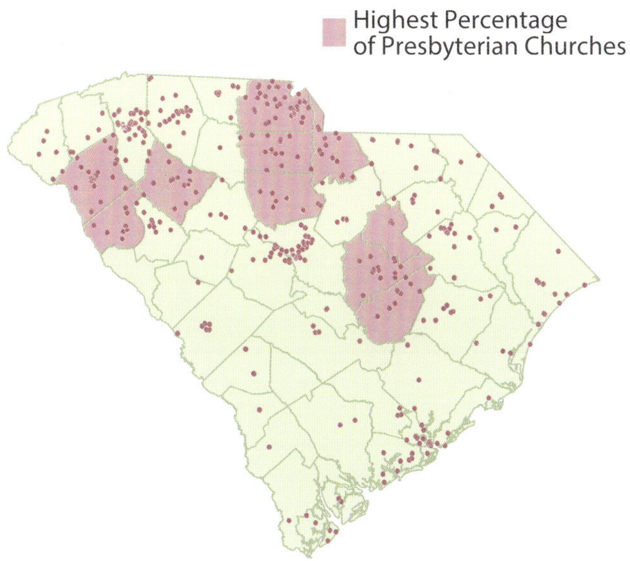

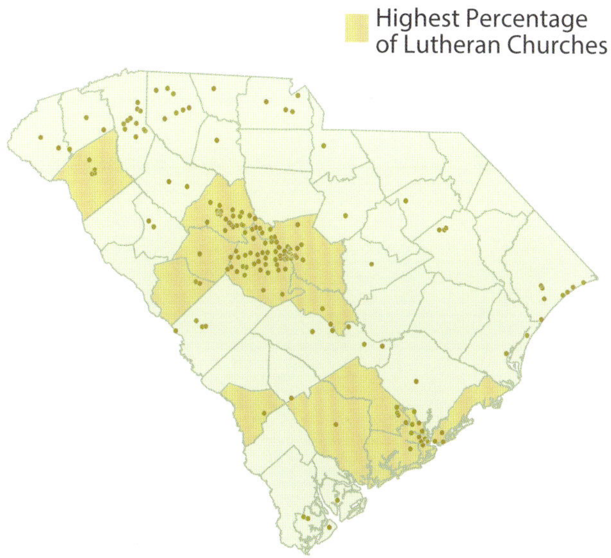

RELIGION

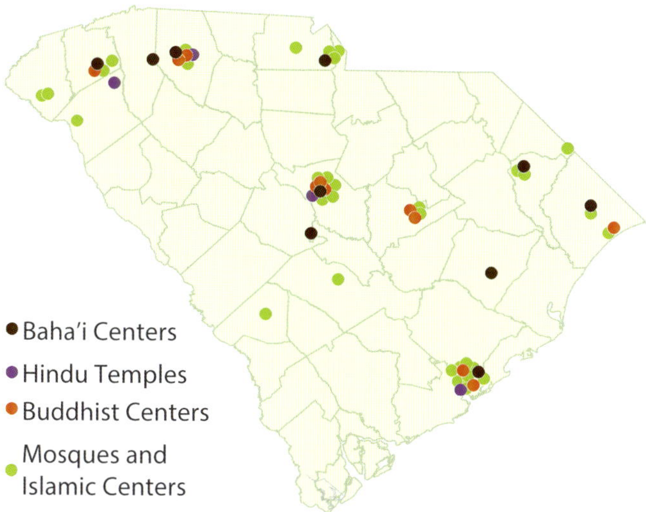

Faiths newer to South Carolina, such as Baha'i, Hinduism, Buddhism, and Islam, tend to concentrate in the state's urban areas. Most of these groups have grown since 1960.

Recent Catholic growth is related to two different migration trends: northern retirees (Horry, Charleston, and Beaufort counties) and Hispanic immigration (Jasper, Saluda).

By 1820 Charleston had the nation's most populous Jewish community. Today, the Jewish population is less numerous statewide and synagogues are primarily located in urban areas capable of support.

Episcopalians are the successors to the Church of England, the de-facto state religion at the colony's founding. Presently their churches are found in larger population centers, but their early Charleston origins are still apparent.

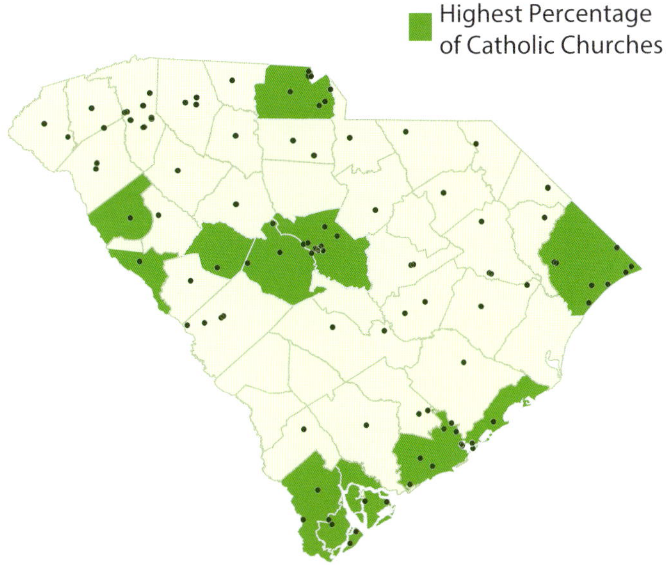

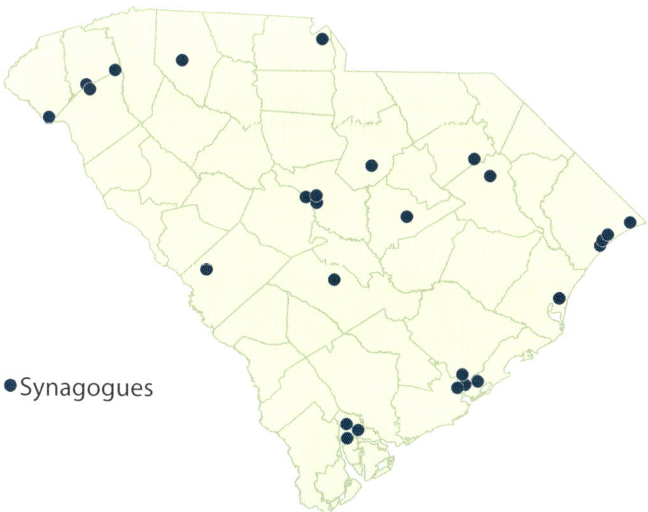

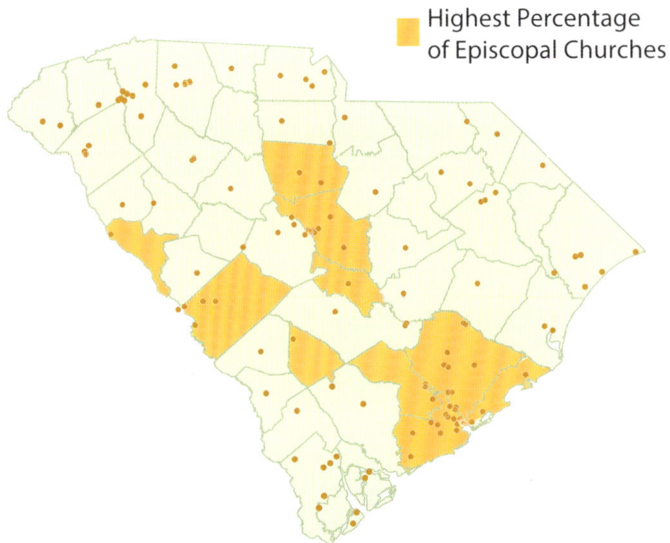

BARBEQUE REGIONS

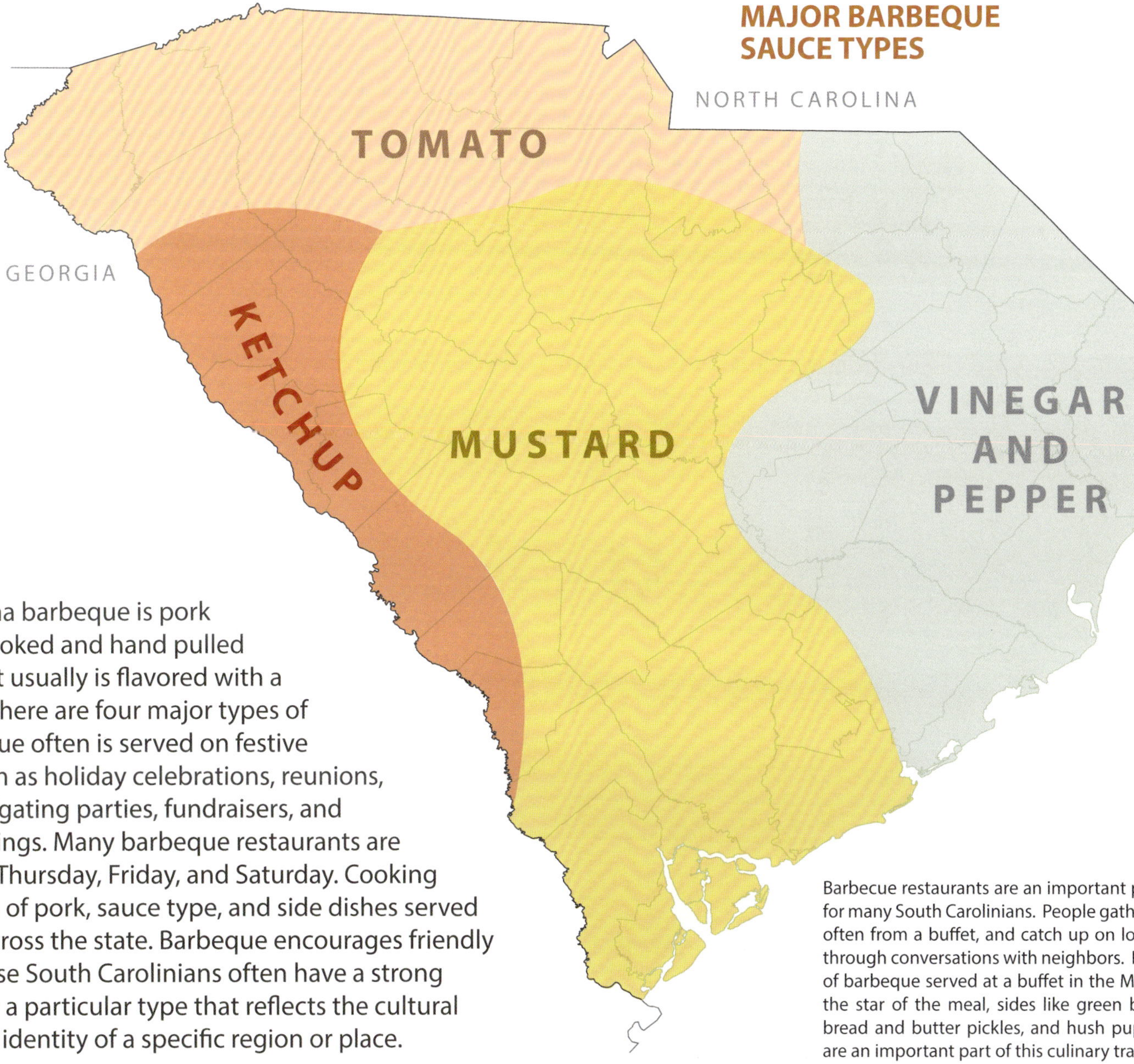

South Carolina barbeque is pork that is slow cooked and hand pulled or shredded. It usually is flavored with a tangy sauce. There are four major types of sauce. Barbeque often is served on festive occasions such as holiday celebrations, reunions, weddings, tailgating parties, fundraisers, and political meetings. Many barbeque restaurants are open only on Thursday, Friday, and Saturday. Cooking methods, cuts of pork, sauce type, and side dishes served vary widely across the state. Barbeque encourages friendly debate because South Carolinians often have a strong preference for a particular type that reflects the cultural character and identity of a specific region or place.

Barbecue restaurants are an important part of the cultural landscape for many South Carolinians. People gather in these spaces to eat food, often from a buffet, and catch up on local news and family updates through conversations with neighbors. Pictured here is a typical plate of barbeque served at a buffet in the Midlands. While pulled pork is the star of the meal, sides like green beans, macaroni and cheese, bread and butter pickles, and hush puppies (fried cornmeal batter) are an important part of this culinary tradition.

COLLEGE FOOTBALL

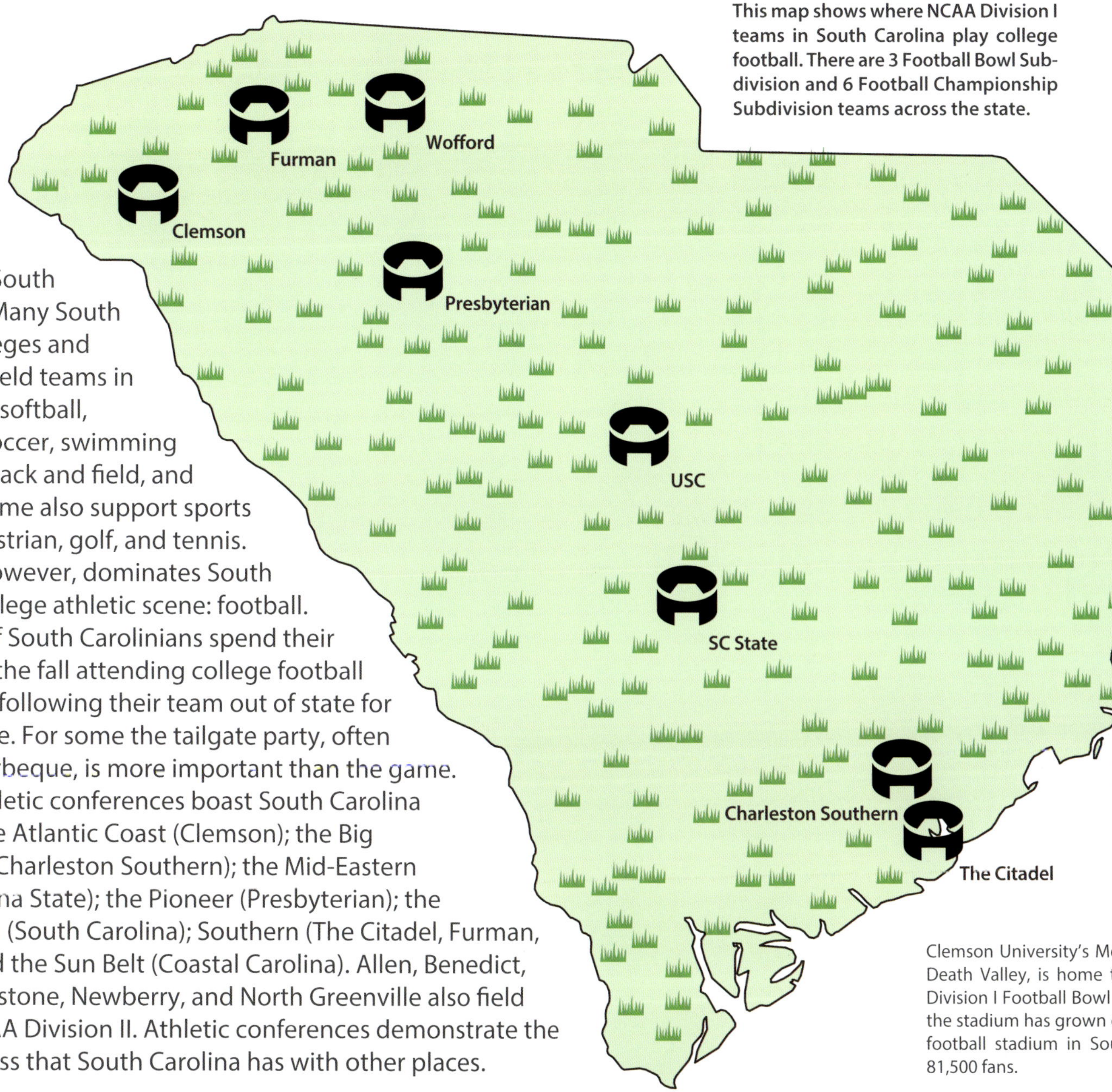

This map shows where NCAA Division I teams in South Carolina play college football. There are 3 Football Bowl Subdivision and 6 Football Championship Subdivision teams across the state.

College sports are actively followed by South Carolinians. Many South Carolina colleges and universities field teams in baseball and softball, basketball, soccer, swimming and diving, track and field, and volleyball. Some also support sports such as equestrian, golf, and tennis. One sport, however, dominates South Carolina's college athletic scene: football. Thousands of South Carolinians spend their Saturdays in the fall attending college football games, even following their team out of state for a "road" game. For some the tailgate party, often with pork barbeque, is more important than the game. Six major athletic conferences boast South Carolina members: the Atlantic Coast (Clemson); the Big South–OVC (Charleston Southern); the Mid-Eastern (South Carolina State); the Pioneer (Presbyterian); the Southeastern (South Carolina); Southern (The Citadel, Furman, Wofford); and the Sun Belt (Coastal Carolina). Allen, Benedict, Erskine, Limestone, Newberry, and North Greenville also field teams in NCAA Division II. Athletic conferences demonstrate the connectedness that South Carolina has with other places.

Clemson University's Memorial Stadium, also known as Death Valley, is home to the Clemson Tigers, a NCAA Division I Football Bowl Subdivision team. Built in 1942, the stadium has grown over time and is now the largest football stadium in South Carolina. It can seat up to 81,500 fans.

ELECTORAL GEOGRAPHY

South Carolina increased its Electoral College representation to nine votes following a population increase between the 2000 and 2010 Census. The state's largest number of votes was eleven from 1813–1840. Its smallest number was zero during secession in 1864. Fifty-nine presidential elections have been held since George Washington was elected in 1789. Over the past ten elections, South Carolina has voted five times for the winning presidential candidate. This map shows the voting pattern for the 2008, 2012, 2016, and 2020 elections. Eight counties flipped at least once between the Democratic and Republican parties. While South Carolina's Electoral College votes over these four elections have all gone to the Republican candidate, this map shows how people voted for different parties in different counties and regions.

ELECTION RESULTS: 2008, 2012, 2016, 2020

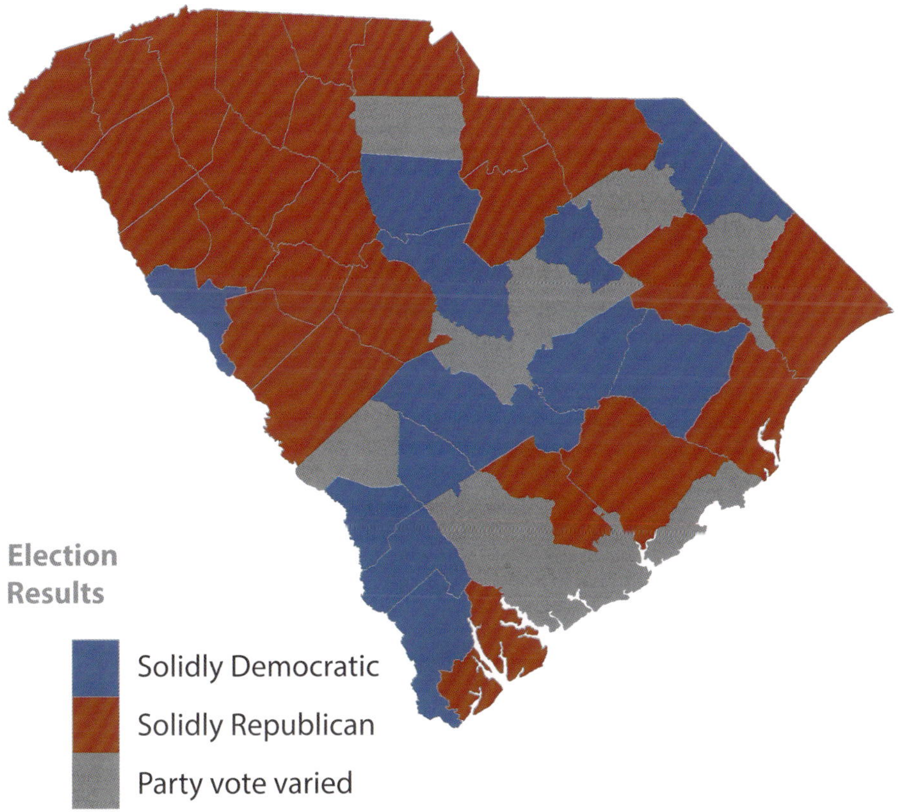

POLLING PLACES ACROSS SOUTH CAROLINA

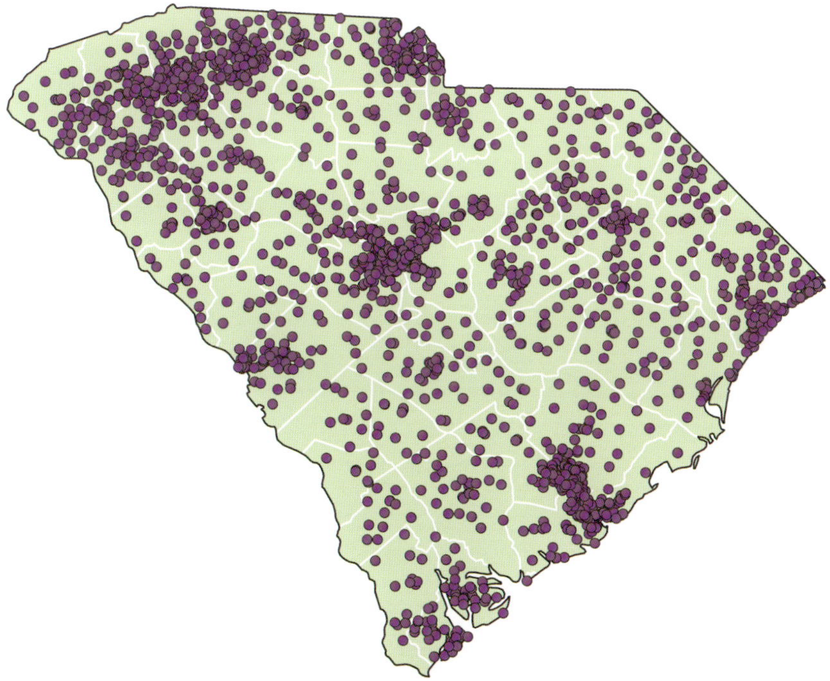

Local, state, and national election outcomes are determined by people who vote at specific local polling places. Typical locations for polling places often include schools, police and fire stations, post offices, places of worship, and local government facilities. These polling places allow the votes of South Carolinians across the state to influence political decisions made at different levels of governments. This map of individual polling places shows how metropolitan areas with more voters have more polling places to accommodate them.

GEOGRAPHIC REGIONS

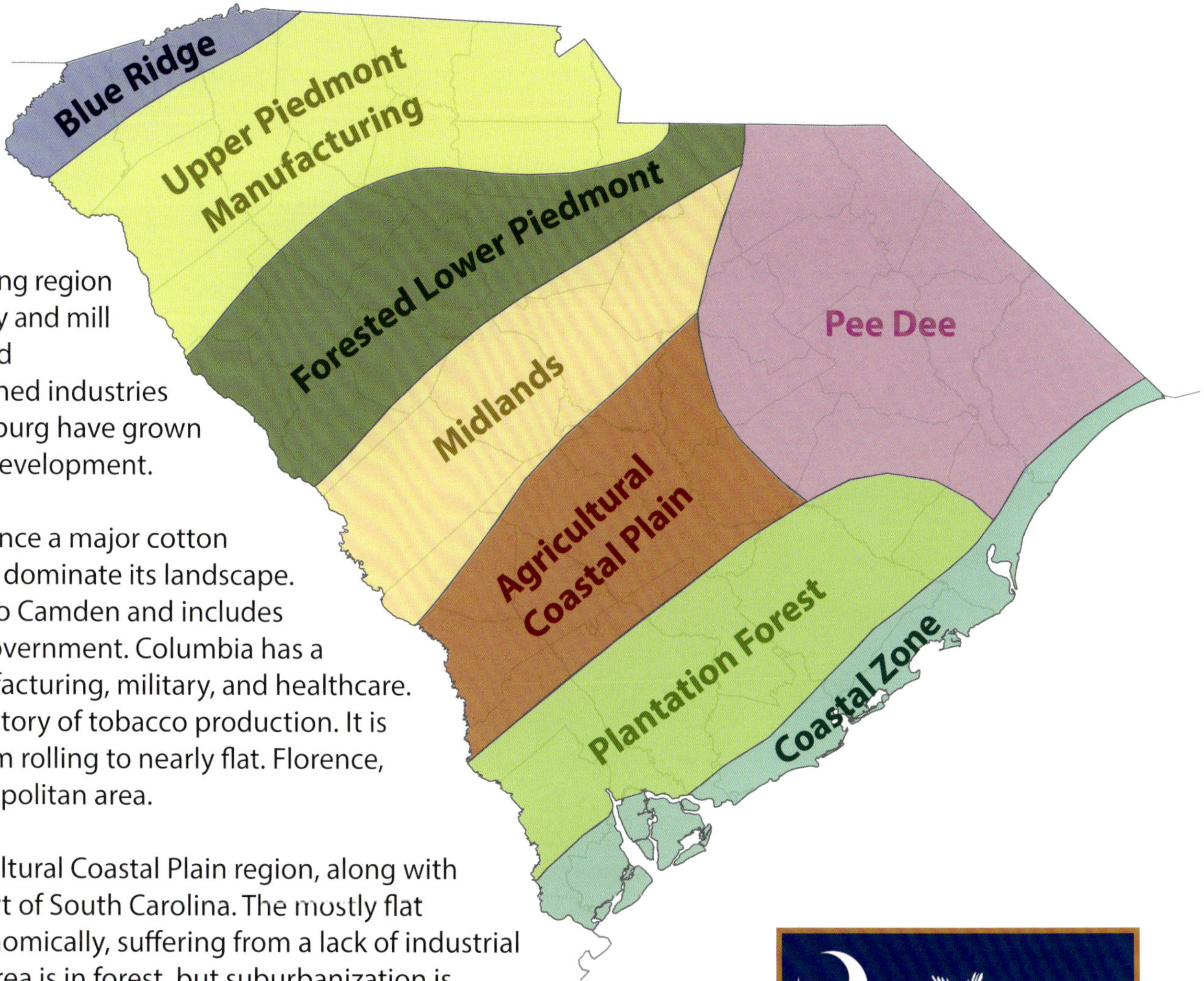

South Carolina can be divided into eight distinct regions based on both its physical and cultural landscapes. The Blue Ridge is a small mountainous area that is sparsely populated but well known for its recreation resources. The Upper Piedmont Manufacturing region used to be identified with the textile industry and mill villages, but recently developed a diversified manufacturing base with many foreign-owned industries along Interstate 85. Greenville and Spartanburg have grown considerably in population alongside this development.

The Forested Lower Piedmont region was once a major cotton producer, but pastures and pine forest now dominate its landscape. The Midlands region stretches from Aiken to Camden and includes Columbia, the capital and center of state government. Columbia has a diverse economy with industries like manufacturing, military, and healthcare. The Pee Dee region is known for its long history of tobacco production. It is largely rural, and its topography ranges from rolling to nearly flat. Florence, originally a railroad hub, is a growing metropolitan area.

The gently rolling topography of the Agricultural Coastal Plain region, along with the Pee Dee, makes up the agricultural heart of South Carolina. The mostly flat Plantation Forest region has struggled economically, suffering from a lack of industrial development. Nearly three-fourths of the area is in forest, but suburbanization is occurring along its coast-side margin. The beaches and golf courses of the Coastal Zone attract North American and international tourists and retirees. Other tourists are drawn to the historic Lowcountry landscape that stretches from Georgetown to Beaufort and is focused on Charleston. Now the state's largest city, Charleston has a fast growing economy and population.

Regions are constantly evolving, and their boundaries move over time and space. Where are you located in South Carolina, and what makes your region unique? What can maps help us communicate about the places we call home in South Carolina?

From the mountains to the sea, South Carolina contains a unique cultural and physical landscape all under one flag.

Tables

Population 1790–2020: Total, Rank, Change, and Density					
Year	Total SC	Rank	Change (%)		Density per square mile
			SC	USA	
1790	249,073	7	n/a	n/a	8.3
1800	345,591	6	38.8	35.1	11.3
1810	415,115	6	20.1	36.4	13.6
1820	502,741	8	21.1	33.1	16.5
1830	581,185	9	15.6	33.5	19.1
1840	594,398	11	2.3	32.7	19.5
1850	668,507	14	12.5	35.9	21.9
1860	703,708	18	5.3	35.6	23.1
1870	705,606	22	0.3	22.6	23.1
1880	995,577	21	41.1	30.2	32.6
1890	1,151,149	23	15.6	25.5	37.7
1900	1,340,316	24	16.4	21.0	44.0
1910	1,515,400	26	13.1	21.0	49.7
1920	1,683,724	26	11.1	14.9	55.2
1930	1,738,765	26	3.3	16.1	57.0
1940	1,899,804	26	9.3	7.2	62.1
1950	2,117,027	27	11.4	14.5	69.9
1960	2,382,594	26	12.5	19.0	78.7
1970	2,590,713	26	8.7	13.3	85.7
1980	3,122,814	24	20.5	11.5	103.4
1990	3,486,703	25	11.7	9.8	115.8
2000	4,012,012	26	15.1	13.2	133.2
2010	4,625,364	24	15.3	9.7	153.9
2020	5,118,425	23	10.7	7.4	170.3

Population and Rank of Largest Incorporated Places: 2020				
Place	Population	2010–2020 change (%)	2020 rank	2010 rank
Charleston	150,227	25.1	1	2
Columbia	136,632	5.7	2	1
North Charleston	114,852	17.8	3	3
Mount Pleasant	90,801	33.8	4	4
Rock Hill	74,372	12.4	5	5
Greenville	70,720	21.1	6	6
Summerville	50,915	17.3	7	7
Goose Creek	45,946	27.8	8	12
Sumter	43,463	7.3	9	8
Florence	39,899	7.7	10	10
Spartanburg	38,732	4.6	11	11
Hilton Head Island	37,661	1.5	12	9
Myrtle Beach	35,682	31.6	13	14
Greer	35,308	38.4	14	16
Aiken	32,025	8.5	15	13
Anderson	28,106	5.3	16	15
Bluffton	27,716	121.2	17	40
Conway	24,849	45.3	18	28
Mauldin	24,724	8.0	19	18
Fort Mill	24,521	126.8	20	41

Published by the University of South Carolina Press
Columbia, South Carolina 29208

uscpress.com

Printed in China

Library of Congress Cataloging-in-Publication Data can be found at http://catalog.loc.gov/.

ISBN: 978-1-64336-626-5 (paperback)
ISBN: 978-1-64336-636-4 (ebook)
DOI: https://doi.org/10.61162/WECC9317

The Open Carolina collection is made possible by the generous funding of the University of South Carolina Libraries.

Page-specific sources, image credits, and resources for teachers and students are available at scgeo.org.
Visit using the QR code below.